ENDORSEMENTS

"Josh Lawson's latest book, *Drugs & Jesus*, approaches a difficult and sensitive topic from a unique perspective that is one part theological reflection, one part personal narrative, and one part reflective commentary from someone with boots on the ground. And while it may seem to cover the topic of addiction, his real subject is the much more taboo: the shame and stigma surrounding drug use. The time he has spent researching data, literature, and the lives of those living with addiction show through his writing. What makes the book stand out are the questions at the end of each chapter. Lawson draws the reader in and engages them with text, drawing upon their lived experience and allowing them to ponder the deeper questions unpinning each chapter. This mechanism draws the reader out of the reading chair with a sense of call and purpose to see how they can respond to his message. My hope and prayer, as a person of faith and as a priest, is that *Drugs & Jesus* makes its way into churches and into the hearts of the faithful."

— **Reverend Paul Bennett**, St. Mary's Episcopal Church of Abingdon

"*Drugs & Jesus* is a moving, warm, beautiful introduction to why harm reduction is not a rejection of faith, but one of its ultimate expressions. Though intended for a Christian audience, it will speak to everyone who has considered ethical questions around caring for people who use drugs and inspire acts of radical compassion."

— **Maia Szalavitz**, Neuroscience Journalist, Author,
Undoing Drugs: The Untold Story of Harm Reduction and the Future of Addiction

"In his latest book, *Drugs & Jesus*, Joshua Lawson gives invaluable insight into the overdose crisis with a keen eye for the role faith can play in its treatment and mitigation. Through the use of story and testimony, along with solid science and sociological evidence, Josh prods the church to rise from its pews of apathy and resignation to be the hands and feet of Jesus to those who have been maligned, marginalized, and marooned by the self-righteous and the self-centered. From the opening paragraphs we are challenged that "for a person's faith to be vital, it must demonstrate itself in tangible acts of love toward those in need." This book is a call to tangibly love those whom we are told are beyond help, to love those whom we are often told are unworthy of our love. No matter your personal experience with substance use or those caught in the terrible grip of addiction, Joshua's words are a timely reminder that this epidemic is not one that the church can afford to excuse itself from. Lives are at stake, and if the statistics are any indication, those lives are more likely than ever to be the lives of people you know and love."

— **Nat Turney**, Co-host, *This Is Not Church* Podcast,
Author, *The Seeds of De(con)struction*

"Josh Lawson gets to the heart of it in *Drugs & Jesus*, or rather he gets to the Gospel of it. Josh reminds us that supporting people who use drugs is not enabling, instead it is the unconditional and transformative love that our faith calls us to. Many of us carry wounds that we have associated with substance use, but Josh asks us to look again and see a bigger picture. What hurts are personal and what hurts are systemic? If you are wondering if naloxone distribution or syringe service programs are in line with your Christian faith, then this is the book for you. Josh ties the healing of harm reduction to the bold and justice-rich example of Christ. Time with this book offered healing to me and to those I love."

— **Minister Blyth Barnow**, Director, HEAL Ohio

"Josh Lawson's book, *Drugs & Jesus,* is a call to action. Better yet, it is a wake-up call to those who have hidden behind rhetoric the church has force-fed us regarding our fellow humans who now find themselves marginalized because of drug use and addiction. Society has divided ideologies regarding drugs to either completely abstain or to join the proverbial "war on drugs". Josh offers a third perspective in his book: harm reduction. Do we dare accept the challenge he presents? We are at a crossroads, and to save the very soul of this nation, we must manifest a new paradigm that does not compartmentalize those individuals who find themselves surviving each day using chemical assistance. Josh deftly expresses the plight of our nation and how we treat people struggling with addiction, and he presents alternatives that can bring about real change. Every pastor, politician, and law enforcement officer should read this book. Every church should use this book as a tool to better understand the drug epidemic in our country, and how they can stand alongside marginalized people within their community."

— **Jon Turney**, Co-Host, *This Is Not Church* Podcast

"Joshua Lawson is a modern day harm reduction prophet in his newest book, *Drugs & Jesus*. This revelation - that we have a spiritual duty to address our own personal stigma about substance use so we can serve the Other with true love, non-judgmental compassion - is a message often missed by abstinence-only based approaches. Lawson succeeds in meeting the reader where they are and journeying with them while providing an opportunity to implement real change in their personal approach when serving people who use drugs."

— **Michelle Mathis**, Executive Director, Olive Branch Ministry

"As a pastor in southern Ohio who is deeply involved in the effort to connect people of faith with those who are suffering from a substance use disorder, I appreciate all that Josh has to say in his book, *Drugs & Jesus*. The scripture he uses to illustrate his points are perfect. People of faith need to gather at ground zero, using every tool available to live into their Baptismal Covenant to heal the sick and serve Christ in all people."

— **Rev. Sallie Schisler**, St. Paul's Lutheran Church

"*Drugs & Jesus* has managed to both water my eyes with tears while at the same time opening them to the call of God's people in our generation. As believers, this book challenges not only what we claim to believe but how we are expressing that belief to the most vulnerable in our society. I believe Josh is calling us to what really counts according to Galatians 5:6, which is 'faith expressing itself through love.' My prayer is this book will move us with compassion to 'get down in the dirt' with others with what Josh calls a 'scandalous grace and radical love.'"

— **Kenny Martin**, Pastor, Lloyd Church of the Nazarene

"As someone who is an advocate for recovery in all areas of life, I appreciate the depth Josh Lawson's book, *Drugs & Jesus*, brings to a very dark place where many become lost and forgotten. So many times recovery is viewed on a surface level where judgment takes over. Without looking deep within ourselves for a better understanding of the struggles that life brings, how can we truly help those who are drowning in their struggles? This book offers a wealth of material which invites us all into a deep meditation on life, scripture, and humanity. I pray that each reader will take time to pause and process this book as they work through it in order to realize that if we want to see change, then the change must start with us!"

— **Rev. Shan Odom**, Host, *The Recovery Pastor* Podcast

"Following up on his ground-breaking debut, *The Face of Addiction*, Josh Lawson has written a deeply personal and intensely spiritual work that leads us away from tired, shame-based religious solutions that often amount to little more than bypassing. Instead, *Drugs & Jesus* helps us learn to recognize Jesus in the 'other' while lovingly calling us to lay down our assumptions about our neighbors who are suffering from addiction. As a former church recovery pastor, I wish I could put this book in the hands of every single church leader I know. Read this book with your heart wide open. When you put it down, you might just have eyes to see Jesus among the poor and addicted where He has always been."

— **Jason Elam**, Host, *The Messy Spirituality Podcast*

"*Drugs & Jesus* is an abundant treasure, which when opened and read provides plentiful resources, solid biblical study, and a thorough exploration of the heart of Jesus for all persons, including those who suffer with substance use disorder. Joshua Lawson helps churches and persons of faith understand the vital importance of harm reduction in order to save lives from opioid overdose. As a clergyperson, this is the very first book I have read that provides real compassion and guidance in this effort."

— **Kristin Santiago**, Lutheran Pastor

"I spent many afternoons and evenings in Joshua's living room as part of the house church he mentions early on in this book. Although my memory is not as vivid or poetic as his, I was there that day when we decided to join the march around Portsmouth's east side to confront the pill mills and express our solidarity with those who were being harmed. Having just read *Drugs & Jesus,* I am so very grateful we decided to attend that march. It has been a great pleasure to bear witness to Joshua's experience of getting to know, advocate for, and simply walk in solidarity with the most vulnerable members of his community in Portsmouth, Ohio. If I can add anything of value to his book, it is this: I can vouch that it is this very experience that has informed and shaped the content of this book. *Drugs & Jesus* is no armchair philosophy, and Joshua is no armchair philosopher. You can be sure that any challenge he offers to the reader is one he has been courageous enough to meet and engage with himself."

— **Andrew Wehrheim**, The Hope Center

"Joshua Lawson's newest book, *Drugs & Jesus*, is a critical and courageous contribution to the movement to eradicate the overdose crisis and help heal the harms wrought by the war on people who use drugs. Lawson draws us into the heart of the crisis by storying its impact on the lived experience of our most marginalized neighbors, calling us to recognize the roots of this crisis, which lay not in drugs but in the stigmatization and criminalization of the people who use them, and the communities in which they live. He invites us to lean past our own understandings and assumptions about substance use, and into the life-giving work of harm reduction and other community-led health and healing efforts. We come to learn about the gospel of harm reduction as faith-full resistance, rooted in love and unapologetically insistent on justice. Lawson invites each of us to follow Jesus' lead and carry this gospel message of dignity, compassion and love to all."

— **Rev. Erica Poellot**, Minister of Harm Reduction and Overdose Prevention Ministries, United Church of Christ

"Josh offers a compelling discussion about how following in the way of Jesus may force us to reckon with an uncomfortable truth: Christ is found in places we don't think He belongs and in the people we deem unworthy. And while he provides practical answers to the implications of this truth, it's his ability to ask the deeper questions about why radical love and compassion can feel so threatening to give (and receive) that makes *Drugs & Jesus* such an important book to read and wrestle with. These words may be hard to hear. Still, he doesn't shy away from laying out the challenge - and all that it might require - because he has enough faith in our humanity to trust that we are up for it. I hope we prove him right."

— **Amanda Klaiber**, RN, Worship Pastor, Christians Beyond Church

DRUGS & JESUS

FAITH MEETS
HARM REDUCTION

JOSHUA LAWSON
AUTHOR OF *THE FACE OF ADDICTION*

Copyright © 2023 by Joshua Lawson, First Edition

Scripture quotations are taken from the *Holy Bible*, New Living Translation, copyright ©1996, 2004, 2015 by Tyndale House Foundation. Used by permission of Tyndale House Publishers, Carol Stream, Illinois 60188. All rights reserved.

Cover design by Rafael Polendo (polendo.net)
Interior Layout by Matthew J. Distefano

ISBN 978-1-957007-59-5

This volume is printed on acid free paper and meets ANSI Z39.48 standards. Printed in the United States of America

Published by Quoir
Chico, California
www.quoir.com

For Christine

CONTENTS

PREFACE

Over the years, I've been privileged to collaborate with many compassionate individuals who have dedicated their lives, vocations, and professional careers to the mission of harm reduction. Much of that work has been faith-based, spanning a generous continuum of spiritual and religious traditions. Unitarian ministers, Muslim imams, Jewish rabbis, evangelical pastors, and indigenous spiritual leaders—far more diversity than this country boy from northern Kentucky ever thought he would comfortably embrace.

Now, I'm guessing that many of my colleagues don't agree on numerous points of religious doctrine, nor do they align perfectly on every matter of social policy. Despite their diverging worldviews, however, they have managed to find a solid piece of shared ground on which to work for the benefit of people who use drugs. This shared ground we call harm reduction.

When I first began writing this book, it occurred to me that the way I chose to frame its message begs a very important question. You might have wondered about it already while reading these opening lines, so let me clarify by asking it myself. When I talk about "faith-based harm reduction," whose faith am I referring to?

The first answer is quite simple: any and all of them. As my own efforts, along with the labor of other faith leaders has demonstrated, the practice of harm reduction does not belong to a single tradition, nor should it be confined to one. The spiritual values that give meaning to this work can be found in practically every religious belief system or spiritual path, from the Bible to the Koran, from the "big book" of *Alcoholics Anonymous* to the *Book of Common Prayer*.

Harm reduction belongs to all of us and none of us at the same time.

My second answer to this question must necessarily be more specific. After all, I am writing mainly from my own point of view and personal experience, which is uniquely Christian. Even that distinction, however, is too broad. To be more specific, my own background within the Christian faith is largely protestant and evangelical – nearly two decades, to be exact – with a few years of progressive Christianity at the end.

Hopefully, this disclosure doesn't scare you away for whatever reason. Whether you favor my background or detest it, I hope you'll stick around until the end of the book. No matter what your personal background, belief system, or affiliation, I truly do believe that the ideas and stories I'm going to share here will serve you well in the end.

As the following chapters will reveal, I believe that people of faith possess a treasury of insight that can give great meaning and value to the mission of harm reduction. In fact, I sometimes have to scratch my head and wonder why there aren't more people of faith engaged in this work to begin with. Have they never read the words of Jesus? The theological basis is undoubtedly there, so I guess the problem is that no one has bothered to pick up the Bible and show them.

Until now.

Before I digress, however, I want to encourage you to really think this message through. Consider the title from Chapter Three, for instance. "Naloxone saves" is more than a catchy slogan, it's a way of saying that for a person's faith to be vital, it must demonstrate itself in tangible acts of love toward those in need. It's not enough to claim that "Jesus saves" while casually stepping to the side of the road to avoid the suffering person on the street in front of you. You must take your faith and put it into a loaf of bread for the hungry child, or a cup of water for the thirsty traveler, or, in this case, a dose of naloxone for the overdose victim.

Then and only then, when our faith comes down out of the clouds and takes form in the world of human suffering, will it have real meaning.

INTRODUCTION

WHAT IS HARM REDUCTION, ANYWAY?

I could hardly believe what I was hearing.

"As much as I support what you're trying to do here, I don't see it working out. That's the thing with drug addicts. You just can't help them."

These words cut right through my heart. To this day, I still tend to sigh when I think of them. I was sitting behind a desk in the secretary's office of the church building where I was pastoring. Across from me sat the church council president and his wife—two of the most ardent supporters I'd had since my tenure with the church began a year and a half prior.

It was cold, as usual. Had the furnace gone out again, or was it just the poor blood circulation in my hands getting the best of me? Hard to say. Either way, the temperature in the room was symbolic. The spiritual vitality had all but drained out of this old congregation; the building creaked and groaned as if bearing witness to the unfortunate fact. There was no denying that the church was in the throes of death.

Why was I there? I had come on board to help them rebuild. Following a decade of declining membership, finances, and community engagement, I was the physical embodiment of what one council member referred to as their last "Hail Mary"—the church's final effort to reignite a spark of spiritual relevance in the community by creating a ministry that people actually cared about and wanted to be part of.

To be honest with you, I was probably both the worst and best man for the job. For starters, it was my first official pastorate, and I had no previous experience in that capacity. But I did have a compelling vision combined with years of formal and informal training. I was already regarded as a faith leader in the community, albeit somewhat of a maverick, and this experience provided many valuable connections. My public work had come to revolve around issues stemming from the opioid crisis, so there was plenty of overlap between what I was already doing in the community and what I could potentially do through the church.

I presented all this to them shortly after signing a part-time contract and beginning to lead Sunday services as "Pastor Josh." I shared my intention to align the church's mission with the recovery community in our town to make the congregation a "church in recovery," building a new, vital ministry around the work I was already doing in support of people who use drugs and those in recovery from a substance use disorder.

That was the plan, at least. And I gave it my very best shot. A year and a half later, though, I was sitting across the desk from my most enthusiastic supporter listening to his despair over the apparent failure of my valiant efforts.

This brother had literally placed his resignation on the table before the church council and told them that if they failed to bring me on as pastor, he was done. Now, despite my best efforts, he finally *was* done. I mustered all the empathy I could in response. The man's family had suffered long and hard due to drug addiction, so his feelings were entirely understandable. At the same time, hearing the resignation in his voice broke my heart. Here I had done everything I could to cast a vision of radical compassion for the outcast in our community, yet the final outcome was more of the same old response: "You just can't help them," he said.

I nodded and smiled faintly, but at that moment, I knew it was over.

Now, I wish I could say this mentality is the exception, but it's more like the rule when it comes to how most people approach the issue of drug use and addiction. Most folks, Christians included, just don't hold out much hope for any individual who is caught in the throes of a substance use disorder. While they may not state it in such explicit terms, this is the quiet, uninformed bias that many of them do hold. And in many ways, this quiet, uninformed bias is just as deadly as outright hostility.

I'm here to tell you a different story, though. I'm here to disrupt your thought patterns and open your imagination to a better approach. You might have heard it said that people who use drugs are too far gone and can't be helped, but I'm telling you that we've not yet begun to tap the endless possibilities of grace. Just as Jesus once stood upon that hill in Galilee and challenged his disciples' self-limiting beliefs, I want to give you a new perspective on the work of harm reduction using language and concepts with which you're already familiar.

Readers of my first book, *The Face of Addiction*, will be familiar with how I originally got into this work, and they will know at least a few stories that humanize the kind of people whom society often places beyond the pale of redemption. I wrote that book to bring you to the edge of involvement; I wrote this one to push you over the edge. I'll hold your hand and try to be gentle, but I'll also expect you to understand that when our neighbors are literally dying to the tune of 128 people per day, the sensibility of the elderly lady in the pew is not my top priority.

So, if you're one of those people who insist that there is only one legitimate path to recovery, such as abstinence-only, getting saved, or [insert your preferred method here], then this book might not be for you.

If you believe that providing access to naloxone and other life-saving tools is wrong because it only enables people to use drugs without discrimination, then this book is going to ruffle your feathers.

If you're sold on the idea of "tough love" because you think the war on drugs is the best way to deal with addiction, then hang on, because I've got some news for you.

However...

If you've ever wondered what you or your faith community can do for people who struggle with a substance use disorder, then this book will help you figure it out.

If you wince every time you hear someone judge, condemn, or stigmatize people who use drugs, then this book will be right up your alley.

And if you sincerely want to get involved in finding solutions to the overdose crisis, but you need a theological framework for your approach to harm reduction, then this book is definitely for you.

If you're like me, then you've probably spent a lot of time—too much time, honestly—with your head in the spiritual clouds. In the following chapters, I'm going to invite you on a journey of theological and practical transformation. Together, we will follow Jesus down out of the clouds into the dirty old earth, where Hell is not just an afterthought reserved for some distant future but the daily reality for multitudes of dying people. If you'll let me, I will show you that one of the best ways to serve God is by engaging in the ministry of harm reduction.

What is harm reduction, anyway? That's a great question. Rather than give you some dry definition right up front, I'd rather let the answer unfold itself before you in the conversation that is to come. If you get to the end of the book and you're still not sure, then I'll consider this project a failure. I don't anticipate that being the case, but just in case you want to peek ahead, the official definition of harm reduction can be found in the appendix.

As we journey together, I'm going to share some statistics that might shock you. I might even slip in a few Bible studies to help you see the opportunity for service that many faith leaders and communities are missing out on. But more than anything else, I'm going to introduce you to *people*—real people who are loved by God, whose lives matter, and who just might scare the hell out of you if they ever did show up to one of your Sunday morning services. Not because they are monsters, but simply because they don't look like you.

In the end, we'll consider a few tangible ways that you and your community can get involved in the business of saving lives. I'll do my best to keep the conversation practical, because I'm convinced that you really do want to believe, despite your deepest fears, that redemption is possible, not just for the saints in the pews but for the sinners in the streets. In your heart of hearts, you know that Jesus saves. You know the old adage is true when it says that God works in many mysterious ways His wonders to perform. I'm just here to show you that harm reduction is one of them.

ONE

FINDING JESUS IN THE "LEAST OF THESE"

"This town... it's ground zero. The pharmaceutical companies
destroyed towns like ours."

— *The Face of Addiction*

"GROUND ZERO." THAT'S WHAT they call it back home.

Portsmouth, Ohio, is widely regarded as the epicenter of the opioid crisis in rural America. This belief hardly represents the entire story behind the current overdose crisis, let alone the addiction epidemic that plagues western society in general, but it is true for a few reasons. Years ago, when certain pharmaceutical companies began targeting geographic areas with vulnerable populations to market their new pain medications, central Appalachia was prime for the taking.

Most of the big manufacturers who once provided living wage jobs for our people had long since left the region for more profitable labor markets. The coal industry was in serious decline, and people were hurting. Like, literally hurting. Supporting a family as a blue collar laborer in the hills of northern Kentucky and southern Ohio does a number on the ole body.

"Pill mills" started popping up everywhere. You could find them in rented store fronts, shopping malls, and even residential houses that had been retrofitted to function as doctors' offices.[1] Typically, these clinics were operated by a doctor who was accompanied by a support staff of nurses and perhaps a few security guards.

One of the first big players in this game was a man by the name of David Procter. Dr. Procter's business model made him a lot of money before ultimately landing him in prison. By the time federal officers caught up with him at the Canadian border, though, he had already taught the next generation of "pill mill docs" how it was done.

Procter was a friend of my family's. My brother and I played on sports teams with his kids and spent the night at his house on multiple occasions. Whenever we were feeling sick, he'd give us free checkups.

I don't remember much about the guy other than feeling like he was a very eccentric and somewhat paranoid person. He had a lake on his property, and he told my dad we could come over and go fishing whenever we wanted. So, we did. I must have been seven or eight years old at the time. Imagine our surprise when gunshots began to ring out just as we set our tackle boxes down on the shore! Apparently, the good doctor saw us from a distance and assumed we were strangers trespassing on his land. My brother and I scattered while dad shouted at him from behind a tree. It took a few rounds before he finally recognized who we were.

Fun times!

Dr. Procter had opened the Plaza Health Center in my hometown of South Shore, Kentucky, in 1979, three years before I was born. By 1996, it had claimed the dubious honor of being America's first pill mill. The business model was simple, really: see as many patients as you can. People came from states away to stand in line outside Procter's office for hours at a time, waiting for their quick diagnosis and prescription. By his own admission, Procter saw 80 patients a day during those years, charging $80 to $120 in exchange for prescription opioids.[2]

Hence the term, "ground zero."

It wasn't long before many of those folks began developing severe chemical dependencies on their new medications.[3] At its peak, Appalachian counties were seeing opioid prescription rates of nearly 120 per every 100 residents, as opposed to only about 70 in non-Appalachian counties. It was the age of quick and easy pain relief. Substances like Oxycontin, Vicodin, and Percocet were championed as the cure-all for a lifetime's worth of back-breaking labor in the coal mines. The problem, of course, was that nobody knew how much suffering was set to follow in their wake. People came to find relief for a back injury and ended up losing their homes and families to a spiraling substance use disorder. The full scope of that devastation is a story for another book, however, a few of which have already been written.[4]

Fast forward about fifteen years, and you'll find a stalwart group of bereaved mothers, concerned citizens, and public health professionals beginning to sound the alarm across the river in Portsmouth, Ohio. In January 2010, Scioto County became the first county in the nation to declare a public health emergency in response to the burgeoning epidemic. Lisa Roberts, a registered nurse at the Portsmouth Public Health Department who was instrumental in leading this charge, refers to that band of early activists as "canaries in the coal mine."[5] They spoke out boldly against the abuse, putting pressure on local, state, and national government officials to intervene amidst the carnage that was being caused by the pill mill doctors.

Portsmouth was literally the frontline in the battlefield of America's rural opioid crisis. Everywhere you look here, there are wounded. As much as I'd like to say that the battle is over and we're just picking up the pieces, the truth is there's still no end in sight.

But that's when my wife and I first stumbled onto the scene. We purchased our first house and moved to Portsmouth that same year. In many ways, we were oblivious to the devastation that surrounded our happy little home. I was leading a small house church that met weekly in our living room. At the time, that little gathering of saints represented the cutting edge of God's work on Earth as far as my little worldview was concerned.

You can laugh all you want, but I'm dead serious when I say that, too—no hyperbole whatsoever. At 27 years old, I was smack dab in the middle of what I now like to call my "wasted years." For me, that season was characterized by a blatant disregard for every other pursuit in life except the realization of what I believed to be God's preferred form of church life.

Dietrich Bonhoeffer called such conceptions a "wish dream," but I called it heaven on earth.[6] To me, the *true* church was a small group of like-minded believers singing classical tunes with re-written lyrics while sharing the Lord's Supper around the dinner table together—fried chicken, anyone? We did that for about four years, and by "we" I mean barely more than a handful of people. We had a few visitors from time to time, but for some reason, no one ever stuck around for long.

There was more to it, of course, but my wish dream is also a story for another book.

For now, I just want you to get a feel for how preoccupied I was with heavenly matters. You know, things like saving souls, building the church, and convincing people of the veracity of my pet theology. Your mileage may vary, but my all-consuming passion in those days was God's "eternal purpose." It was a compelling vision, mind you, but it was all up in the clouds for me, a metaphysical dream in which I got lost for the better part of a decade.

If you're familiar with the phrase, "tunnel vision," then you know that's what I had. I didn't possess my beliefs so much as they possessed me. My eye was "single" for Christ and the church – nothing else mattered. All while people just down the road from me were suffering in a veritable hell-on-earth due to corporate greed, bad social policies, and other debilitating issues that I had no clue about.

While I was busy playing church, people were dying. But then I saw Jesus for the first time with a needle in his arm, and everything began to change.

Now, I know that might sound strange, but if you'll spare me a few more moments of personal indulgence, I want to tell you how it happened. I need to risk boring you with a few more snippets of my house church journey (a mini movement where we "churched" in our living rooms instead of in a building) in order to do so, though, because the main point won't come across quite as effectively without the historical context.

So, travel back with me.

It was a Saturday. The sun was shining bright above my little three-bedroom house on Grandview Avenue. The birds were singing just outside the window, and my heart was soaring. I was off work, which was rare for a Saturday, but this day was special because the church was hosting a very special friend of ours from out of town.

Dave was standing in my living room, all decked out in his button up shirt, blue jeans, and old-man slippers, holding a freshly brewed cup of coffee.

Dave was part of a network of churches that were much like our little group, meaning they were small, their meetings were informal, and they, too, believed themselves to be at the cutting edge of God's work in the world. The only difference was that they had a lot more experience than we did. They were part of a fellowship with origins stretching all the way back to mainland China in the early 20th century. Their network included many groups spread out over multiple states, and this brother was one of their recognized leaders. As such, he spent most of his time traveling and ministering to the churches in their network.

Shortly after meeting Dave on a trip to western Ohio, he came to see us in Portsmouth. That first visit had been epic. We packed the house with as many people as we could get to share a meal, sing songs, and encourage one another. Anticipation was in the air. Dave talked to us about the vision of Christ and the church in a way that made me feel like we had stepped right back into the book of Acts.

At the end of the night, I sat across the couch from Dave with another brother and discussed our future. Dave committed to regular visits to help build us up, just like the apostle Paul did in the first century when he would "lay the foundation of Christ" among a group of new believers.[7] Apparently, our little gathering impressed Dave enough that he felt it was worth the gas money to keep coming back.

Smiling wide, he said, "I can't wait to get back home and tell the other saints about how the Lord is working among you here in Portsmouth."

I tried to contain myself, but I'd be lying if I said I didn't feel like a kid on Christmas morning. It was late, and I was tired from the day's activities, but my heart was on fire. To me, this was divine validation, the fulfillment of my deepest dreams. Nothing mattered next to Dave's affirmation. I felt like those Galatians when Paul first visited them, so enamored with his presence that they would have plucked out their own eyes to give to him if necessary.[8]

True to his word, Dave began to visit us once a month. Every Saturday we spent together was great, but the only visit I distinctly recall other than that first apostolic jaunt was his final trip to Portsmouth. That was the day when God interrupted my glorious wish-dream to show me just how much my neighbors were suffering.

As usual, we were all gathered at my house when Dave arrived. Hugs and handshakes were exchanged, with gusto as always. Out came the slippers and coffee. Then someone asked, "What should we do today?" since we hadn't really planned for anything special. My best friend and his wife, who had been part of the church since the beginning, suggested we go take part in a march that was happening in town that afternoon. Apparently, some folks from the community were planning to walk through Portsmouth's East End—the notoriously rough side of town—to hold a demonstration in front of the pill mills that were located there.

I didn't like the idea one bit. I wanted to do what we always did—sit around the house talking, praying, and singing about heavenly stuff. What did this "march" have to do with God's eternal purpose? Why would we waste the one precious afternoon we had with our apostle-like leader to go walking around the trash-ridden streets of Portsmouth's East End?

Of course, I said none of these things. I've never been one to insist on my own way, and we were big on group consensus in those days, so when the others seemed to go along with the idea, I rolled with it. I was disappointed inside, though. Deeply disappointed.

Nevertheless, we piled into our cars and drove across town, where we found a group of people assembled at the corner of the block. Climbing out of the car, I recognized a few faces but not many. Clouds had gathered overhead on our way there, and it looked like it might rain. A slight chill descended on the air.

Certain individuals held posters with pictures and messages written on them—photos of people who had died of an accidental drug overdose. We stood and waited awkwardly. Finally, a few people took turns speaking to the crowd. One of the speakers was a public health worker; another, a local faith leader. Someone said a prayer, I think. It seemed like the atmosphere was reflected in the weather—mostly somber, with a few rays of light streaking through the clouds here and there.

At last, the march began, and we slowly made our way through the streets. The clouds opened along the way, so we lifted our umbrellas to shield ourselves from the rain. Residents peered at us from their windows as we trudged by. Cars slowed to a stop or pulled over to let us pass. I still didn't know exactly what we were doing there, but the more we walked, the more my feelings of resentment melted. Looking around, I began to see things that I hadn't noticed before.

I saw young kids playing on the sidewalks, seemingly oblivious to the pain that surrounded them, although the discontented look in their eyes said otherwise.

I saw old mothers walking together, their arms wrapped tightly around each other as if cradling their broken hearts.

I saw the tear-stained photos of dead sons and lost lovers clutched close to their chests.

And I saw fire in the eyes of the organizers. Undeniable fire. Maybe it was the same fire I'd felt in my own heart back on the couch at my house, I wasn't sure. But one thing I could tell: this flame wasn't dancing aloft somewhere up in the clouds of an ethereal spiritual reality. This fire was born of pain, and it was rooted in the earth.

As we finally made our way back to where we began, having circled numerous blocks throughout the neighborhood, a rainbow appeared in the distance. Many of the marchers looked up and smiled. A few people snapped pictures. I felt it was a nice ending to an otherwise inconvenient day.

Then I noticed something else.

Across the street from where we stood, getting ready to hop back in our cars and return to church-life utopia, I noticed a ramshackle old house. Through the broken glass of the picture window on the front of the building, I saw in my mind's eye a man. Utterly alone, slumped over in a chair with a needle in his arm.

There was no one else around. His figure was stark and shrouded in darkness. Gaunt. Empty pop cans and crumpled chip bags lay scattered on the floor around him. The white of his eyes barely visible under upturned lids. For all I knew, he could be dead or dying.

A wave of sadness washed over me. Somewhere out there, someone had a history with this man. Be it his mother, a child, or perhaps just a friend, someone loved this brother with all their heart. And that someone would give anything to have him back. To them, he was beloved.

I shuddered as I suddenly realized that this man was not one person but many—the nameless, faceless epitome of the opioid crisis. I recoiled at the sight, for he was every stereotype I had ever learned about a person who uses drugs. Yet in that moment he became something more. As I gazed deeper into the darkness of that abandoned old house, his appearance was transfigured before me, and I saw the man for who he really was.

The slamming of a car door recalled my attention. I shook myself and looked around; my friends were ready to go. Turning to leave, I cast a final glance at the house across the street. Then I heard a familiar refrain inside me—the words of Jesus echoing in my heart as if for the very first time.

"Truly I tell you, Joshua, whatever you do for one of the least of these brothers and sisters of mine, you do for me."[9]

QUESTIONS FOR REFLECTION

Perhaps you're familiar with the old saying, "Don't be so heavenly minded that you're no earthly good." Reflecting on this sentiment, can you identify a time in your life when you fell into this trap? What does it mean to be so heavenly minded that you're no earthly good? How can you avoid this predicament?

_____

_____

_____

_____

_____

_____

_____

_____

_____

_____

Do you personally know someone who uses illicit drugs? When you think of that person, what feelings and images arise in your mind? Forget everything you're *supposed* to think about them and reflect instead on your most honest, visceral feelings about their relationship with drugs.

_____

_____

_____

_____

_____

_____

_____

_____

_____

_____

Have you ever experienced anything like the author's mystical "vision" at the march? Perhaps it wasn't an instantaneous revelation but a gradual insight. How did that experience help shift your mindset?

_____

_____

_____

_____

_____

_____

_____

_____

_____

_____

_____

How do you understand Jesus' words about the "least of these" in Matthew 25? How might this understanding apply to your current or past mindset about people who use drugs?

_____

_____

_____

_____

_____

_____

_____

_____

_____

_____

_____

TWO

WILL THE REAL FAITHFUL PLEASE STAND UP?

"Talking about any of this is hard for me in general. I'm currently struggling, you know. Trying to find my place in the world. I don't think that place exists, though."

— **Chris,** *The Face of Addiction*

AS YOU PROBABLY KNOW, Jesus and his disciples were Jewish. Most of the people they interacted with every day were also Jewish. Geographic limitations aside, the general scope of Jesus' ministry seemed to be intentional. We know this because Jesus went on record saying that his mission was specifically targeted at Jewish people and no one else.[1]

Sometimes, though, Jesus and his crew would run into *other* people, whom they called Gentiles. These were the non-Jewish peoples of the ancient Roman world. A Gentile could be Samaritan, Cappadocian, Arabian, or Parthian. It didn't really matter. The main distinction with these folks was that they weren't Jews. For this reason alone, some Jewish people referred to them as "dogs."

Before you poo-poo such derogatory language, however, you should know that the Master himself wasn't averse to taking this line of speech. I'm not saying that makes it right. It's not like you should ask, "What would Jesus do?" and then go call your neighbor a dog. I'm just saying that even the best of us can get caught putting stigmatizing labels on other people. Even divinity, at least when it takes human form, is subject to cultural distinctions of time and place.

Despite Jesus's own apparent humanness, however, he had a fascinating way of transcending his cultural heritage. This transcendence can be seen in the way he routinely led his disciples into seemingly chance encounters with the Other—people whom his Jewish followers naturally considered to be *outside* the covenant blessings of God.

Take that Syrophoenician dog, for instance. You remember her, right?

The story is found in Matthew 15. Jesus and his crew were traveling through the region of Tyre and Sidon when a local Canaanite woman cried out for him to help her ailing daughter, saying, "Son of David, have mercy on me!"

Now, I'm betting that you also remember the story of David and Goliath in the Old Testament. Goliath was a Philistine, aka a *Canaanite*, who defied the army of Israel. When none but the young shepherd boy was courageous enough to meet the giant in battle, King Saul sent David to confront Goliath in the valley.

Seeing David approach with just a staff and a sling, Goliath roared, "Am I a dog, that you come to me with a stick?"[2]

"Am I a *dog*?"

"Son of *David*, have mercy on me."

I'm assuming there's some theological connection here between that ancient Jewish story and Jesus' encounter with the Canaanite woman. Because when Jesus refused to answer her repeated pleas, even to the point that his disciples became visibly annoyed, he finally replied, "It isn't right to take food from the children and throw it to the *dogs*."[3]

Ouch.

But this is where the story takes an interesting turn, for the woman's cunning reply seems to stop the Master dead in his tracks.

"That's true, Lord, but even the dogs are allowed to eat the scraps that fall beneath their master's table."[4]

I imagine Jesus abruptly stopping and raising his eyebrows at this point. Turning to her, he says, "O woman, great is your faith. May you have what you desire." Scripture claims that her daughter was healed that very hour.

Now, there's some really important stuff in this story about stigma. I want to look at that for a minute before we get back to the original point. Here, we see Jesus passing through unfamiliar territory. A non-Jewish woman (an Other) whom most Jews regard to be outside the covenant blessings of God which they alone enjoy—comes to Jesus asking for help.

First, Jesus ignores her, refusing to even recognize her presence. When she continues to cry out and begins to make a scene, he acknowledges her presence but refers to her as a dog—in other words, something other than human. Then finally, when she arrests his attention with her cunning response, he calls her "woman."

By reverse engineering this simple exchange, we learn how the process of dehumanization takes place. This happens all the time with people who use drugs, you know. First, we refer to them as something other than or less than human.

Addict.

Junkie.

Pill head.

Eventually, the use of stigmatizing language desensitizes us to the point that we feel justified in ignoring their need—and sometimes, even their existence—altogether. Then, we can act as if their lives are expendable or that they are someone else's problem.

Whether Jesus was intentionally playing with words in this story, using the well-known prejudices of his people to make a point, or whether he himself learned a valuable lesson from the Canaanite woman, is a question for a different book. Evangelicals and progressives like to debate the possibility, but for this conversation it doesn't matter one way or the other. My point is simply to show you how the process of dehumanization takes place, how it can be reversed, and how this is one striking example of Jesus leading his disciples to see the value and humanity of an Other.

It seems like he was doing this all the time, actually. For another example, let's drop back a few chapters in Matthew's Gospel. In Matthew 8, we find the story of a Roman centurion whose servant was sick.

Jesus was traveling through Capernaum when the centurion came out to meet him. Upon hearing about the condition of the centurion's servant, Jesus said he would go heal him.

The centurion raised his hand, objecting.

"Lord, I am not worthy to have you come into my home. Just say the word from where you are, and my servant will be healed. I know this because I am under the authority of my superior officers, and I have authority over my soldiers. I only need to say, 'Go,' and they go, or 'Come,' and they come. And if I say to my slaves, 'Do this,' they do it."[5]

Perhaps Jesus raised his eyebrows at this statement. Perhaps he tilted his head to the side in surprise. Scripture simply says that he marveled. Turning to the disciples, he said, "I tell you the truth, I have not found this kind of faith in all of Israel!"[6]

Full stop right there. Listen to what Jesus is saying.

Looking right into the eyes of his disciples—his *Jewish* disciples, mind you, who steadfastly believe that the covenant blessings of God belong to them alone as children of Abraham, and that the Gentiles, whom this centurion is, live in spiritual darkness with no light from God whatsoever[7]—he says, "I tell you what, guys, I've yet to see this kind of faith from anyone in Israel!"

It's a mic drop moment if ever there was one.

Seriously, if you're struggling to grasp the full import of Jesus's words in this passage, think of it this way: Imagine that the God of all glory took human form once again and moved into your neighborhood. Then, he picks *you* to be one of his disciples. *You*, who've been a churchgoing, tithe-paying, Sunday-school-attending Christian all your life. How exciting!

So, you begin to follow him around town. One day, he encounters a woman on the street, a local sex worker who shoots heroin and hasn't darkened the doorstep of a church building since she was a little girl. She begs the Master to heal her sick son and he agrees, but then she says something to the effect of what that Roman centurion said to Jesus back in Century One.

With his face glowing, the Son of God turns to you and says, "Did you hear what she said? That was awesome! I haven't found this kind of faith anywhere in the whole church! You guys don't hold a candle to the simple, child-like faith this girl possesses."

How would you feel at that moment? Surely, it must be similar to what Jesus' disciples felt when he led them to encounter an Other in the form of the Roman centurion. I have to believe the Lord got a real kick out of doing this, if only to see the look on their faces.

There's a moral to this story. I hope you're already getting it. In case you're not, let's take a step back and view the subject through a wider lens.

What I'm trying to do here is give you a theological framework for why you should and how you can approach the Other—in this case, people who use drugs—in a way that will bring healing rather than harm. As a person of faith who holds the Bible in high esteem, have you ever considered how much ink was spilled in the writing of scripture to show God's people that God is just as present and active among folks outside their circle as God is with them?

The prophets emphasized this truth constantly, which, coincidentally, is why so many of them ended up getting killed. They liked to point out how God's plan extended well beyond the people of Israel. Yes, God may have established a special relationship with Abraham, but that was not so Abraham's lineage could keep all those divine blessings to themselves, but so that the blessing of the covenant could flow through them to the *entire world*.

Everyone. Including the Gentiles. The universal Other.

If you're like me, you've probably glossed over some of the more radical things the prophets said in this regard. Amos, for instance, said this to the people of Israel in the name of Yahweh:

"'Are you Israelites more important to me than the Ethiopians?'" asks the Lord. 'I brought Israel out of Egypt, but I also brought the Philistines from Crete and led the Arameans out of Kir.'" [8]

Did you catch that? Prophesying *in the name of the Lord*, Amos says that God brought the Philistines and Syrians out of bondage into their land just like God brought the Israelites out of Egypt.

What?!

That's right, and it gets even better. In fact, this passage from Amos is the very one that James quoted at the Jerusalem council when the apostles and elders came together to consider the question of Gentile inclusion in the church.[9] The miracles God accomplished through the ministries of Peter, Paul, Barnabas, and others were enough to convince James that the witness of scripture was true, and that God's activity was not confined to the Jewish nation alone. Turns out the Gentiles—those *Other* people—were in on this, too!

The entire trajectory of scripture is toward the radical love and inclusion of the Other—all those people whom we previously thought to be outside the circle of God's favor. Write it in stone. End it with a period. Drop the mic and walk away.

This truth that the prophets insisted on proclaiming even to the point of death is precisely what gripped me that Saturday afternoon in Portsmouth, Ohio. By leading me into an unexpected encounter with a ragtag group of community organizers, God interrupted my cozy little wish dream with a vision of Jesus in the least of these, bedraggled with a needle in his arm.

My slumber was comfortable and carefully circumscribed. For years, I had been headed sharply in one direction—straight for the clouds—but then suddenly the road forked, and God placed a bypass right in front of me. In the words of John Henry Newman, "I sought to hear the voice of God and climbed the topmost steeple, but God declared: 'Go down again—I dwell among the people.'"

This was my personal experience, of course, and I expect no one to take it as a model for their own. I'm not claiming that everything I did back in those days lacked any practical value whatsoever, just as I'm not insinuating that about your work now. I'm simply saying that I hope to be for you what those bereaved mothers were for me—a divine messenger of sorts, loud enough to get your attention, and committed to the task of showing you that God is active in the field of harm reduction.

Maybe you've been taught to believe that the one and only life-saving message is contained within the four walls of your church, and that the only hope an individual has for salvation is to find their way inside. But you might be surprised to learn that God is out there in the streets and in the homes of people who use drugs, and that they possess faith too, perhaps even a faith that is greater than your own.

Regardless, you should know that Christ has identified himself with people who use drugs in a very special way. The invitation of the moment is not theirs, in fact, but yours. Jesus is inviting you to recognize his image and serve him in the Other, and that includes the person with a needle in their arm.

Will you accept his invitation?

QUESTIONS FOR REFLECTION

If you were in the shoes of the disciples and Jesus said to you, "Look at this woman's faith, it is far greater than your own," how would that make you feel? What would your response be?

_____

_____

_____

_____

_____

_____

_____

_____

_____

_____

_____

How does it impact your theology to consider that God was just as interested in bringing other people out of bondage as he was with ancient Israel? Have you ever noticed Old Testament passages that speak of non-Jewish people in this way? What is your reaction to the idea of God having people outside the church that may be just as much "God's people"?

_____

_____

_____

_____

_____

_____

_____

_____

_____

_____

_____

Think of someone in your life who would fit the description of being the "Other." How do you relate to that person currently? Are there ways in which your relationship with that person may be dictated by uninformed prejudice?

_____

_____

_____

_____

_____

_____

_____

_____

_____

_____

_____

Consider the process of dehumanization that we "reverse engineered" from Jesus' encounter with the Syrophoenician woman. What other types of people in addition to those who use drugs are often dehumanized in our society, whether past or present? Describe the steps that are taken to overlook, dismiss, or otherwise reject their humanity.

_____

_____

_____

_____

_____

_____

_____

_____

_____

_____

_____

THREE

NALOXONE SAVES!

"I understand harm reduction to be an act of unconditional
love. I think it is how we love our neighbors. For me, harm
reduction is the work of the Gospel."

— Blyth Barnow

WE CHRISTIANS FACE TWO problems when it comes to the Other. The first
problem: we don't understand them. The second problem: we think we do.

These problems apply overwhelmingly to people who use drugs.

Historically, churches tend to speak to their communities more than they
listen to them. People of faith assume the moral high ground by default
because we think we have all the answers. But we don't. Especially when it
comes to things we don't understand. This subconscious blindness is why
humility—which is the general posture of servanthood—was one of the
prime characteristics Jesus wanted his followers to possess.

"Take the lowest seat at the table," he said. "In the Kingdom of God, the
first will be last and the last will be first."

"Seek to serve rather than be served. Even the Son of Man didn't come to
be served." "Love one another. Love your neighbor as yourself. This is how
everyone will know you are my disciples."

Radical, unconditional love sounds nice in theory, but it often gets lost in translation when we seek to apply it to real-world scenarios. This is why we have to be very specific about what it means to love other people, or in this case, those who use drugs.

Loving people starts with listening to them. We must listen so that we can learn. What makes them tick? What causes them pain? What forces have shaped their lives? How was their upbringing different from ours? What motivates them to get out of bed in the morning? How do they understand themselves and their own choices?

Until you can begin to answer these questions from the other person's point of view, you'll never be able to effectively serve them, regardless of how much you think you know about their situation.

For Christians who believe in one universal problem—sin—that has one universal answer—salvation—this fact is easy to overlook. But the complexity of human experience should teach us that there is no one-size-fits-all solution to any problem. As much as we hate to admit it, there is no cookie-cutter approach that can be applied in every situation.

Therefore, it is imperative that we listen to our neighbors. By listening to them, we can learn how to love them. And I don't mean the kind of listening that is just waiting for your turn to speak. I mean an *active, conscious, attending to the self-expressed needs of other people.* This kind of listening is the essence of genuine love, for as Simone Weil said, "Attention is the rarest and purest form of generosity."

Now, another story.

In the summer of 2019, my church hosted a special memorial service for people who had died of an accidental drug overdose. It was the week of August 31st, International Overdose Awareness Day. Every year, this day is observed by individuals and organizations across the world to raise awareness about overdose and reduce the stigma surrounding people who use drugs.

I was pastoring a small, United Church of Christ congregation that year. Don't ask me how I went from leading a house church in my living room to pastoring a mainline congregation with custom stained-glass windows because I don't have time to tell you that story right now. But there I was, the man behind the pulpit. I was working hard to align the church's mission with our local recovery community, so when the opportunity arose to host Blyth Barnow, Harm Reduction Coordinator for Faith in Public Life Ohio, I jumped at the chance.

Blyth was conducting a tour of churches across the state that week in honor of Overdose Awareness Day. The format for her service included prayers for lost loved ones, special music, the lighting of candles in their memory, a brief message about the value of faith-based harm reduction, and a training on how to use naloxone.

Naloxone is more commonly known by the popular brand name Narcan, which is its nasal spray form. Naloxone is an opioid overdose reversal medication. In other words, it's a miracle drug. Literally, a life saver.

When a person injects an opioid, the opiate binds to certain receptors in their brain. Typically, this binding process results in quick pain relief, a general sense of well-being, and in some cases, a sudden rush of euphoria. In the event of an opioid overdose, however, the substance taken is either too much or too strong. Consequently, the person's respiratory system slows to dangerously low levels. They lose consciousness, their lips turn blue, and they stop responding to external stimuli.

Would you know what to do if you witnessed a person overdosing?

Now, let's say there is someone on hand who can administer naloxone. If it's Narcan, they simply insert the nozzle in the person's nose and spray. The medication immediately goes to work, reversing the process of overdose, causing the opioids to "unbind" themselves from the brain's receptors. The person goes into withdrawal and wakes up.

Instead of dying, they *wake up*. Kind of like a resurrection. Can you see the theological significance?

It is precisely this theological significance that led Blyth to name her service, "Naloxone Saves." You might think the phrase sounds like a spoof of the popular evangelical proclamation, "Jesus saves," but I assure you it is no spoof. Not at all. Rather, it is an affirmation of the supreme value of faith-based harm reduction.

Do you wish to serve Christ in the least of these? Do you want to save lives? Then carry naloxone. Learn how to recognize the signs of overdose and be ready to respond when it happens. Yes, Jesus saves, but so does naloxone. What better way to practice your faith during a national overdose crisis than to distribute and carry this life-saving medication?

The Naloxone Saves service was beautiful. I can't go on without telling you about it. We held the event on a Thursday evening to coincide with the Narcotics Anonymous (NA) meeting that was happening in the church basement around the same time. I spoke with the NA leader prior to the event, inviting the group to come upstairs after their meeting. Those who accepted the offer were given a free naloxone kit and shown how to use it if they didn't already know.

Now, I've attended thousands of church services over the years, most of which I recall nothing about. But this service, which was part memorial and part field training, stands out. After lighting a candle in memory of those whose lives had been lost to overdose and the War on Drugs, Blyth shared a poignant message of hope. She told us how to recognize the signs of drug overdose and what to do in an emergency. Then, in old-school, high-church fashion, she blessed the naloxone.

"Creator of resurrection and light," she said with hands raised, "we come to you with grateful hearts for all the ways your love continues to rise up in our midst. We give you thanks and praise for the holy drug, naloxone, and the new life that it can bring."

Shifting in my seat like a kid who can't keep his eyes closed during the pastor's prayer, I cast furtive glances this way and that way, attempting to gauge the reactions of people in the pews around me.

"We know that we need each other to survive," Blyth continued, "so we ask you to bless these kits, and all those who will use them, and all those who will be in need of them."

My attention was drawn to a woman a few rows in front of me. Her shoulders were bobbing slightly, and she had one hand placed over her mouth, weeping.

"Make them and us instruments of resurrection," Blyth said, "that suffering will be released, that injury will be transformed, that joy will arise, that strength will take hold, that hope will take wing, and that death will yield to new life."

That death will yield to new life. The words sang in my heart.

"Empower us to live in our vocations as people of resurrection, bringers of new life, proclaimers in word and deed of a new day rising. In the name of all that unfurls hope in our midst every moment, we pray. Amen."[1]

Glancing around the sanctuary, I saw many somber expressions. A few people were smiling lightly, nodding their heads in affirmation. The woman two pews up was still crying. Blyth invited us to come to the altar and take as many kits as we needed. The service ended on this note.

The only thing that mattered to me in that moment was talking to the woman up front. More than anything else, I wanted to know who she was and what she was feeling. As folks began to shuffle out of their pews, I stood in the aisle and waited for my opportunity. Finally, it came.

"Hey, I'm Josh, the pastor here," I said.

The woman threw her arms around my shoulders. Her eyes were red, but she was smiling.

"Thank you so much for doing this," she said. "I've been in treatment now for three weeks. Just this summer, I overdosed twice on heroin. I wouldn't be alive today if someone hadn't been there with naloxone to save my life."

"That's incredible," I said, stepping back from her embrace. "I'm so glad to hear that."

Tears welled up in her eyes as she nodded vigorously. "I didn't think I was going to make it," she said, "but now I have a chance. Now, I get to be here for my daughters. I'm getting better for them and for me. You don't know how much it means to people like me...to see a church doing this. Thank you so much."

You know, I understand how tempting it is to believe that there's nothing you can do to help people who struggle with a substance use disorder. Especially if you've been burnt more times than you can count by someone you love. But the story doesn't end there. It *can't* end there. Giving in to the voice of despair and writing off millions of people simply because you've been hurt by one or two is the easy way out. Taking this position is akin to asking God, as Cain did long ago, "Am I my brother's keeper?"

The answer to Cain's question is yes, by the way. Christians and humanists alike should be able to agree on this proposition. We are here to take care of each other. To love our neighbor as ourselves. To give people the benefit of the doubt despite their checkered past. Why? Because we believe in the power of grace and the possibility of redemption.

So, every time you're tempted to despair, remember this: there's a woman out there right now who is enjoying her life in recovery. She is taking care of herself while providing for her children. She's living one day at a time, taking each step with gratitude for the second chance she was given in life. All because there was someone nearby in her moment of need who cared enough to know how to recognize and respond to an accidental overdose.

Don't tell me it's not possible. I don't have time for such limiting beliefs, and neither do you. You might have heard it said that there is nothing you can do to help people who have a drug addiction, but I'm here to remind you that you've been called to practice resurrection. Your mission, should you choose to accept it, is to offer the world a radical love that extends far beyond the limits of human possibility.

This is what faith-based harm reduction is all about.

QUESTIONS FOR REFLECTION

Think about the church or congregation to which you belong. Do you spend as much time listening to the needs of your community as you do speaking to them? How might the rhythm of your church look different if you listened more than you spoke?

_____

_____

_____

_____

_____

_____

_____

_____

_____

_____

_____

Simone Weil said that "attention is the rarest and purest form of generosity." When someone approaches you with an important concern, how often do you find yourself shaping your own response instead of genuinely listening to what they are saying? What value would it bring to your relationships if you learned to practice more active listening?

_____

_____

_____

_____

_____

_____

_____

_____

_____

_____

_____

What thoughts, images, and feelings came up for you as you read about the blessing of the naloxone?

_____

_____

_____

_____

_____

_____

_____

_____

_____

_____

_____

How do you understand the theological significance of the woman in this chapter who shared about being revived from an accidental overdose by someone with Narcan? Can carrying naloxone be a tangible expression of resurrection faith? Could this be a symbol or sacrament for you and/or your faith community? Why or why not?

FOUR

AMAZING GRACE, HOW SWEET THE SOUND

"At that point, I was shooting up. I hit a vein and registered blood. But I was done with life that night. I tried to push the needle in and kill myself – what they call a hotshot. But it wouldn't go in. So, I registered again. Blood came out and I pushed, but it wouldn't go in. I tried a third time, and when it didn't go in again, I said, 'I hear you, God'... I dropped the needle and got on my knees. The next morning was Sunday, so I got my tennis shoes and put on my little dress and took off looking for a church."

— **Denice,** *The Face of Addiction*

THE SMELL OF SWEAT and hardwood fills the air. My teammates are seated around me, beat down from a tough first half but determined to win the contest. The voice of my high school basketball coach is reverberating against the cold metal lockers.

"God helps those who help themselves," he says, looking each one of us dead in the eye. "If you want something, you gotta work for it. No one's gonna come along and give it to you."

Fair enough, Coach, I think to myself. *We've gotta take responsibility and get the job done here. I get it.*

Coach Ward was known for his witty one-liners, but this was one of his favorites. In fact, he repeated these words more times than I could count during my three years under his tutelage.

You want to be a good basketball player? *God helps those who help themselves.*

You want to win this game? *God helps those who help themselves.*

You want to get good grades in school? *God helps those who help themselves.*

You want to make something of yourself in life? *God helps those who help themselves.*

The idea that God helps those who help themselves is a common refrain in Central Appalachia. It's one of many ways that Southern Conservatives express their belief in personal responsibility. For what it's worth, I like it.

And yet.

Even as a teenage boy, I knew there was something slightly off about my coach's little zinger. While I could fully appreciate the idea of divine assistance arriving in response to my self-initiative as a motivational tool, I was conscious enough to realize that this was only half the story at best.

Personal responsibility is invaluable, but it's only one side of the coin. Social responsibility is the other side, and it's the one you need to consider in relation to harm reduction. Assuming personal responsibility means doing whatever it takes to "pull yourself up by your bootstraps"—a well-known conservative adage with which you might be familiar. But social responsibility is about making sure everyone has access to a pair of bootstraps in the first place.

Telling poor folks to pull themselves up by their bootstraps when they don't even own a pair of bootstraps is unhelpful. By the same token, you won't improve the lives of people who use drugs by telling them to "just say no" or else you're going to let them die alone in the street.

So, maybe you've heard it said that God helps those who help themselves, but I'm telling you that divine grace meets people exactly where they are long before they ever lift a finger to help themselves.

This principle lies at the bedrock of Christian theology, you know. Theologians call it "prevenient grace"—the idea that God shows love and favor toward humans *prior to* any response (or non-response) on their part.

Remember what the apostle Paul said? "God showed his great love for us by sending Christ to die for us while we were still sinners."[1] Then there's the writer of 1 John, who said, "We love God, because God first loved us."[2] And in the gospel of John, Jesus put it like this: "You have not chosen me, but I have chosen you."[3] In all three instances, the idea is the same: grace always comes first.

In other words, my coach had it backwards. It's not, "God helps those who help themselves," but, "God helps people so they can help themselves." God gives us grace which then enables us to change. When you look at it this way, it's easy to see why theologians also refer to "prevenient" grace as *enabling* grace. We'll come back to that term, "enabling," in a few chapters, but for now I simply want you to understand that the only thing harm reduction enables a person who uses drugs to do is stay alive.

I also want you to see the mind-blowing correlation between the Christian teaching of divine grace and the core philosophy of harm reduction, which is *meeting people where they are.* These two principles are literally one and the same.

"Meeting someone where they are," writes Dawn Perez, "means bridging the gap between your own expectations and where the other person is coming from. It means intentionally listening to understand their values, needs, desires, and even their trauma-responses."[4]

Meeting individuals where they are seems like a simple and straightforward approach to life, but most of us fail to practice it because we are too busy making judgments about people, especially those *Other* people. Generally, we tend to approach folks with preconceived judgments about who they are and what we think they need.

Tell me this isn't the case with drug use and addiction. I dare you.

When it comes to people who use mind-altering substances, each individual has their own reason for why they do so. For those whose lives have become unmanageable through a substance use disorder, there is often a whole constellation of factors playing into their drug use. And yet, when it comes to these people, you probably already think you know what they need, don't you? You know exactly what they need to do—just stop using drugs and get "clean"—right?

But this is a moral judgment, and a moral judgment is fundamentally different from a genuine assessment. You can't help someone while you're judging them, and you'll never know how to help someone until you've entered a relationship and gotten to know them on a personal basis. Until you meet them where they are, all bets are off.

Now, let's consider this principle in light of the popular AA/NA concept of "rock bottom." The gist of this idea is that an individual with a substance use disorder will not seek or benefit from help until they've reached their absolute lowest point. No matter how much you care and no matter how hard you try, there's nothing you can do to help until their life becomes so miserable that they have nowhere else to go but up.

Rock bottom teaching is used to validate the criminal justice approach to addiction as well as many personal decisions that an individual might make to stop "enabling" the behavior of their loved one. Advocates of this theory believe that until the costs of drug use outweigh the rewards of drug use, the person using drugs will never change their behavior.

Of course, there's a nugget of truth in this assumption because all genuine change is self-determined; therefore, until a person is ready to move in a different direction, there is little one can do to force them otherwise. However, this fact does not mean that they can't be helped in the meantime. Realistically, there's all kinds of things you can do to help someone who isn't ready to change. The way some people talk about "rock bottom," though, would make you think otherwise.

Am I right, or am I right?

The problem, then, is not so much the concept itself but how it can be misapplied. Just because someone has a problem with their drug use (and not all people who use drugs do have a problem) doesn't mean you should make their life as miserable as possible to force them to change. Nor should it justify social policies that eliminate safety nets, destroy families, and create barriers to housing, life-saving medications, and other forms of assistance that people so desperately need.

Cain probably would have been a fan of rock bottom teaching. In fact, I can hear him now: "Sorry, Lord, but until Abel hits rock bottom, there's nothing I can do for him. Am I my brother's keeper?"

Of course, the whole idea of rock bottom is entirely subjective. No one knows where that point of decision will be for another person. My breaking point is probably different from yours and vice versa. Everyone is different; therefore, it's up to each individual to decide when they are ready to change. So, while I understand the intent and acknowledge the partial veracity of rock bottom teaching, I can't accept it being used to avoid the social responsibility I have toward my neighbor. There is no doubt that the buck ultimately stops with them, but there's plenty I can do to help them out in the meantime.

Enter harm reduction.

Meeting people where they are, regardless of whether they seem to have reached their personal bottom, has never been more important than it is now. In the age of illicit fentanyl (more on that in a minute), there is one clear and identifiable rock bottom looming just around the corner for every person who uses drugs: death. And when you hit *that* bottom, there's no coming back.

No redemption.

No recovery.

No happy ending.

Just a trail of broken relationships and bitter tears, at the end of which lies a cold, hard monument to the failure of tough love.

Yes, tough love.

I'm not trying to step on any toes here, so please don't take it that way, but most folks who champion the idea of rock bottom do so based on a belief in what they call "tough love." This approach is characteristic of conversative American culture. Tough love advocates believe that doing too much for another person will make them overly dependent on outside assistance. You can't keep bailing people out when they make the same bad choices over and over again, they say, or else they'll never learn their lesson. Eventually, you just have to let them suffer the consequences of their decisions.

Again, there's a kernel of truth in this belief, and that's what makes it so appealing, especially to social conservatives who were born and bred on the idea of personal responsibility. It is true that you can't live someone else's life for them, especially if you want them to grow strong and learn how to stand on their own two feet. This is why it is important for individuals who are close to someone with a substance use disorder to maintain healthy boundaries for the good of both parties, so they don't enable destructive patterns of behavior in either themselves or their loved one.

But these are two very different matters. Personal boundaries should not equate to social policy. Just because it's not a good idea for grandma to keep giving money to her grandson when she knows he's using it to buy heroin doesn't mean that subsidized housing shouldn't be accessible to people who use drugs.

Regardless of what you've been told, harm reduction is not the same as enabling, and tough love is not always the best approach. If you don't believe me, just ask the guy who got beat up on the road to Jericho.

I'm guessing you know Jesus' parable of the Good Samaritan. It represents yet another instance of Jesus being all sneaky with his storytelling—getting his listeners to admit that it was the "Other" who was doing God's will by being a good neighbor to the person in need.

Don't you ever wish that Jesus would just let sleeping dogs lie? Am I the only one who ever reads scripture and thinks, *Darn it, Lord, why can't you just let me be comfortable in my prejudices?*

No? Just me? Ok.

Anyway, the parable of the Good Samaritan was a story Jesus told in response to a man who was an expert in Jewish law. The guy had asked Jesus what he should do to inherit eternal life, to which Jesus responded by asking his belief. The lawyer gave a typical orthodox answer which Jesus affirmed: "Love the Lord your God with all your heart, soul, strength, and mind, and your neighbor as yourself."[5]

But the man didn't stop there because he was fishing for validation. "Who is my neighbor?" he asked. And at that point, Jesus told his story.

> "A Jewish man was traveling from Jerusalem down to Jericho, and he was attacked by bandits. They stripped him of his clothes, beat him up, and left him half dead beside the road. By chance a priest came along. But when he saw the man lying there, he crossed to the other side of the road and passed him by. A Temple assistant walked over and looked at him lying there, but he also passed by on the other side. Then a despised Samaritan came along, and when he saw the man, he felt compassion for him. Going over to him, the Samaritan soothed his wounds with olive oil and wine and bandaged them. Then he put the man on his own donkey and took him to an inn, where he took care of him. The next day he handed the innkeeper two silver coins [6] telling him, 'Take care of this man. If his bill runs higher than this, I'll pay you the next time I'm here.'"[7]

I like to imagine Jesus recounting this parable rather nonchalantly, perhaps walking in a semi-circle, glancing around at people in the audience as he spoke. Then at the end, when it came time for the punchline, he circled back to the lawyer and locked eyes with him, saying, "Now, which of these three, do you think, proved to be a neighbor to the man who fell among the robbers?"

Of course, there was only one obvious answer to this question, so the lawyer gave it. "The one who showed him mercy," he said.

Nodding his head, Jesus replied, "You go and do the same."

Boom. Roasted.

Now, let's apply the lesson of this parable to everything we've talked about so far. First, notice a few things about the story. The main subject is a man. He has no name, no nationality, no class, no nothing. He's just a human being in need. Never mind the fact that he was traveling a road by himself that was well known to have bandits lurking around every corner. Seems a little irresponsible if you ask me, but Jesus made no point of that.

The man gets jumped, beaten up, robbed, and left for dead. Not a great day. Lucky for him, though, a few religious people were also out and about and ended up encountering his bloodied mess of a body on their way.

Jesus claims that this encounter happened "by chance." That's a little tongue-in-cheek of the Master, don't you think?

Anyway, the two people who first passed by were a priest and a Levite—two members of the religious elite who were alleged to be in close contact with the Most High God. Instead of stopping to help the poor guy, they crossed to the other side of the road and passed by, treating the fellow as an inconvenience at best and non-existent at worst.

Then came a Samaritan. Oh no, it's the *Other*! I can just see the foreheads of the people in the crowd wrinkling at this imaginative turn of events. And what did that nasty old half-breed do when he encountered the man in need? Why, he stopped! He felt compassion toward the man, and he allowed that compassion to *move him to action*. Instead of crossing to the other side of the street like the priest and Levite before him, he stooped down and treated the man's wounds with oil and wine. Then he transported him to the nearest place of shelter, spent the night at his side, and wrote a blank check for his medical care in the morning.

It's no wonder we call him the "Good" Samaritan.

Notice how Jesus reversed the lawyer's original question with this parable. The man had asked Jesus, "Who is my neighbor?" but after telling the story, Jesus asked, "Who was a neighbor to this man?"

It's as if Jesus was saying, "Sorry pal, but you're asking the wrong question. And when you ask the wrong question, you always get the wrong answer. The question is not, 'Who is your neighbor?' but 'Who are *you* going to be a neighbor to?'"

Think about that one for a minute.

There was one point to Jesus' parable, and it was this: If you really want to possess eternal life, you'll love God with all your heart and love your neighbor as yourself. And if you're unsure what it means to love your neighbor as yourself, the answer is very simple. Whenever you see someone in need, help them.

Don't blame them for getting themselves into such a mess. Don't take it upon yourself to point out what decisions they should or should not have made to avoid the harms they are now experiencing. Don't dismiss yourself from social responsibility like Cain, and don't pretend there's nothing you can do until they reach some yet-to-be-determined "rock bottom."

No, the Master will have none of that foolish talk. If you really do care about your neighbor, then you will go and do the same thing that Samaritan did. You won't cross to the other side of the road and pretend that people who use drugs don't exist. You won't dismiss the person with a substance use disorder as unworthy of your care. You won't allow yourself the easy luxury of believing that they are beyond the reach of redemption.

Why won't you do those things? Because you know that God's grace really *is* amazing. And you're beginning to see how that grace aligns perfectly with the practice of harm reduction, which is to meet people where they are and serve them in that place.

No judgment.

No expectations.

No strings attached.

And above all, no sermonizing about how God helps those who help themselves.

Only faith, hope, and love. Only genuine kindness that is born of your heartfelt trust in the radical, compassionate love of God.

QUESTIONS FOR REFLECTION

In this chapter, we learned that harm reduction is all about "meeting people where there are." With this concept in mind, describe some ways of "helping" people that do *not* look like meeting them where they are. Where has the church failed to meet people where they are? How can you begin to show this kind of love toward people who use drugs?

_____

_____

_____

_____

_____

_____

_____

_____

_____

_____

_____

Think about a time in your life when you applied "tough love" and/or "rock bottom" ideology to your relationships. In what ways was this approach helpful? In what ways was it unhelpful? How has this chapter enabled you to re-examine those concepts?

_____

_____

_____

_____

_____

_____

_____

_____

_____

_____

_____

Reflect on the simple truth that recovery is only possible if an individual is still alive. Knowing this, why do you think so many people still resist the idea of harm reduction?

_____

_____

_____

_____

_____

_____

_____

_____

_____

_____

_____

_____

When we read Jesus' parable of the Good Samaritan, we often imagine ourselves in the role of the hero. But has there ever been a time in your life when you showed up as the anti-hero, playing the scribe or Pharisee instead of the good Samaritan? What beliefs were driving your motivation in those times?

_____

_____

_____

_____

_____

_____

_____

_____

_____

_____

FIVE

AREN'T WE JUST ENABLING PEOPLE TO USE DRUGS?

"To enable is to kill."

— D.C. Hyden

"No WAY. THERE'S NO way I would give twenty dollars to someone if I knew they were in active addiction. Twenty dollars' worth of heroin can kill a person."

I looked at the guy talking and then at the person he was addressing. The tension hanging in the air between them was palpable. I was seated to the side, moderating a panel discussion between five participants—all of them in active recovery from substance use disorder—and a room full of faith leaders.

The intent of our conversation was to explore how the church had either hurt or helped people seeking recovery. To this end, we had assembled a group of concerned clergy and congregants to hear from folks with lived experience about how faith communities could better serve people who use drugs.

During the discussion, someone brought up the topic of harm reduction. One of the audience members mentioned the importance of approaching people without judgment and with no strings attached. As an example, she said that if someone asks her for twenty dollars and she can help them, she will give them the cash, no questions asked. No background checks, no personal reference requirements, and no lectures about how they should or should not use the money.

That's when the guy on the panel interjected. In no uncertain terms, he made it clear that while he appreciated the non-judgmental sentiment, there still had to be limits on the kind of help one gives to a person who is at risk of an accidental overdose. In his opinion, giving them cash would be crossing the line because chances are good they would use it to buy drugs. And he wasn't about to do something that might contribute to someone else's death.

Now, before we go on, let me ask *you* a question. Between these two people and their respective opinions, which one do you relate to the most?

Let me guess—it's the guy, right? The one who said, "It's important that we don't go too far and inadvertently enable people to use drugs."

I mean, it is a good point, isn't it? After all, isn't the whole message of this book about finding ways to reduce the harm being experienced by people who use drugs?

To which I would say, "Yes, *but*."

Now, you might be experiencing your own "Yes, but..." moment at this point in our journey. You may be thinking to yourself, *Ok, Josh, I get it. I see there is a theological basis for harm reduction. I need to stop assuming I have all the answers and just meet people where they are with basic, life-saving services. I'm with you on this much, but my conscience is still bugging me. How far is too far? If we give people Narcan to reduce their risk of dying, won't that enable them to use drugs without discrimination?*

If you're not thinking something like that at this point, then kudos to you. But mark my words, eventually you'll meet someone who does. This question comes up all the time among those who don't yet see the difference between harm reduction and enabling.

Maybe you're an idealist who believes that abstinence is the only viable path to recovery and the only moral solution to substance use. Or maybe you've just got some lingering doubts based on an outdated worldview that you're struggling to shed. Either way, I'd like to try to answer those questions of conscience for you in this chapter. Because although you might have heard it said that harm reduction just enables people to use drugs without discrimination, I'm telling you that the only thing harm reduction enables a person to do is stay alive.

And as we've already discussed, that's kind of a big deal.

John Galsworthy, a British author who lived and wrote at the turn of the 20th century, said that "idealism increases in direct proportion to one's distance from the problem." That's a penetrating insight, isn't it? Basically, it means that the farther away you are from an issue, the more rigid your understanding of it will be.

From a distance, preventing drug use seems quite simple. "Just say no," we tell our kids, citing the latest horror story about that high school football star who threw his life away for a fun time. They might nod their head as if they understand the point, or maybe just to get us to shut up. Either way, we pat them on the head and walk away, satisfied that we've done our part to stem the tide of illicit drug use.

From the other side of the room, it might appear to be quite clear what that person with an addiction needs to do. "Just stop using," we say. Isn't it obvious? Well, to you, maybe. But you're failing to account for all the unresolved trauma that is trapped inside their body, driving them to repeat learned behaviors over which they feel they have little to no control.

And to those in recovery who are struggling with thoughts of relapse, we blithely admonish them toward abstinence. "Don't pick up," we remind them. Easy peasy. Problem solved. To which they are probably thinking, *Thanks a lot, Captain Obvious.*

Do you see how easy it is for an armchair theorist to solve other people's problems for them? Idealists are always offering simple solutions to complex problems. That's why, from a mile away, the overdose crisis appears to be far simpler than it really is. To an idealist, it always comes down to other people accepting for themselves what seems obvious to the idealist. And if the world refuses to conform to the idealist's limited view of reality, then they simply wash their hands of the matter and place all the blame where it rightly (in their opinion) belongs—on the other person.

Of course, there's nothing inherently wrong with having your own set of standards. We've all got personal beliefs and ideals that we hold to. But your personal ideals belong to you and not the guy down the road. This is why it's so important, as we've already discussed, to be continually listening to and learning from the Other—people whose lived experiences and worldview are vastly different from your own.

Maybe you would never stick a needle in your arm, no matter how bad life got. Wonderful! Good for you. I'm happy to know you were taught effective coping skills that have kept you out of harm's way in this respect. But what about the woman who grew up in the foster care system? She never had a stable family environment to call her own. Even worse, she was molested repeatedly by those who were supposed to take care of her. And nobody ever taught her how to regulate her nervous system when the suffering became unbearable, so now she's living with the effects of post-traumatic stress disorder.

For all you know, that shot of heroin she's chasing represents everything she didn't get to enjoy as a distressed child: an imaginative escape from a dark, scary world; or a soft, warm hug from someone who cares about her. Comfort. The very thing that faith communities could, and should, be providing to people in need.

But you'll never see these things from a distance. You'll never get to know the nuance and complexity of her situation if you keep her at arm's length. From the other side of the room, all you can offer her are well-worn platitudes and idealistic diatribes about what you're certain she should and should not do to solve problems which you know nothing about.

In many ways, harm reduction starts with a firm commitment on your part to "just say no" to this blockade of idealism. It means giving up your easy answers and meeting people where they are, so you can accompany them on their own healing journey. Not as their savior, but as their friend.

Why am I harping so much on idealism? Because "rock bottom" is an ideal. "Tough love" is an ideal. And your conviction about not "enabling" people—at least when it prevents you from providing basic life-saving services to those who use drugs—is also an ideal. Although each of these concepts represent a partial truth that holds value in certain situations, once solidified into an ideal, they become an impenetrable barrier to the help that many marginalized people desperately need.

You remember the woman from chapter three who finally made her way to treatment after multiple overdoses because someone saved her life with Narcan? What if that other person had believed in tough love and refused to carry Narcan because they thought it would just enable people like her to use drugs? What if that sweet mother had died instead of being given a second, third, or fourth chance at life?

You don't want that on your conscience, do you? I know you don't, which is why we're having this conversation to begin with. That's why you relate to the guy who feared giving twenty dollars to someone in active addiction because he didn't want to chance contributing to their death. Your heart is in the right place when it desires to do no harm. I'm just here to smooth out the rough edges of your conviction by showing you that things like naloxone distribution and fentanyl test trips are part of the solution, not the problem.

Ah, yes, fentanyl test strips. What are fentanyl test strips and why are they so important, you ask? That's an excellent question. To answer it, you should know a little more about fentanyl itself, so let's break it down.

The overdose crisis that is currently rocking the United States is a direct result of the proliferation of fentanyl in the illicit drug supply. Pharmaceutical fentanyl is a synthetic opioid that is approved by the federal government for treating severe pain. Fentanyl is like morphine, with which you might be more familiar, only fentanyl is *50 to 100 times more powerful* than morphine. Most doctors prescribe it to manage the extreme discomfort people feel after surgery or during cancer treatments. If you've ever received fentanyl from a medical provider, you probably experienced it as a shot, a patch on your skin, or a lozenge.

But that's the pharmaceutical type. The illicit stuff is made in clandestine laboratories by rogue chemists who sell it on the black market as a white powder. This powder can be smoked, shot, or pressed into pills that look just like other prescription opioids.

Like any synthetic opioid, fentanyl acts by binding to the brain's opioid receptors. The only difference, once again, is that it does its work far more quickly and powerfully than other opioids. First, it chases your pain far, far away. Then, it releases a chemical explosion of euphoria that saturates your body and mind.

So far so good, right? But then comes the trick, because if you take too much, you might slip into a state of blissful unconsciousness and

never

wake

up.

The driving force behind the overdose crisis is the fact that illicit fentanyl is being cut in almost any substance you can think of, including non-opioids like cocaine, ecstasy, and methamphetamine. Only it's being mixed *without the knowledge of the person using the substance*. Or it's being pressed into pill form and sold as a common prescription painkiller like Vicodin or Percocet.

Theoretically, you could go out on the street today and think you are purchasing run-of-the-mill heroin when, unbeknownst to you, you're actually getting something far more powerful. Your drug dealer isn't deceiving you on purpose to try to kill you (at least, most of them aren't), he's just trying to hook you with a more potent product.

You see where this is going, though, don't you? You take that baggie with the white powder home and prepare to shoot up. Thinking you've got heroin in your possession, you inject an amount you believe you can handle. Only it's not heroin, it's fentanyl, and by the time that Herculean substance is flowing through your veins, it may already be too late. You begin to nod off. Your breathing slows. Your lips turn blue. Before long, it's game over.

This is why it is more important than ever to put fentanyl test strips into the hands of people who use drugs. In less than 30 seconds, a person can use these strips to determine with a high degree of accuracy whether the substance they are preparing to ingest contains fentanyl.

That's the simple magic of harm reduction. By providing fentanyl test strips on the front end to help prevent an overdose and naloxone on the back end to help reverse an overdose, you've just enabled your loved one to stay alive for one more day. And who knows what joy, what redemption, what recovery, that day might bring?

Now, to the point of this chapter.

These passionate admonitions of mine aren't meant to imply that you should always give cold, hard cash to anyone who asks for it. But they are urging you to support practices and policies that will keep people alive and healthy despite any choices they make which you may not agree with. And please, for the love of both God and your neighbor, stop conflating harm reduction with enabling, because they are not the same thing.

When I say that harm reduction is not the same as enabling, I'm trying to articulate the difference between how we relate to people on a personal level—when, for instance, someone close to us is stuck in destructive patterns of behavior—and how we choose to support the general well-being of our neighbors through effective social policies.

In other words, I have a specific reader in mind when I say that harm reduction is not the same thing as enabling. I'm envisioning a mother or grandmother who has learned through painful experience that giving their child a hundred dollars to help with "rent" every time they come back asking for more money is not the best way to support them and may be doing more harm than good.

This person may subconsciously equate such relational "enabling" with the free distribution of Narcan or clean syringes when, in fact, these two practices are worlds apart. One deals with the painful reality of personal experience, including the legitimate need for healthy boundaries and calculated relief efforts. The other deals with society's general approach to people who suffer with a substance use disorder, and how we should cast the social safety net as wide as possible in order to do the most good for the most people.

So yeah, there is a genuine sense in which harm reduction *is* enabling people to use drugs. But we're talking about people who are going to use drugs anyway. If it helps, think of it this way: providing Narcan, fentanyl test strips, and clean syringes is a way of supporting the *people* who use drugs rather than the drug use itself. It is our way of saying, "We care about you, and we want what is best for you. If you decide you want to make changes in your life, we're here to support you in that, too. But in the meantime, we want you to be as safe and healthy as possible, because you are valuable to us, and your life has purpose. No strings attached."

That's what I mean when I say that harm reduction is not the same thing as enabling. If anything, it is enabling people to *live*, in the hope that they will find their way to healing and wholeness through whatever means necessary. That's the message. That's the point.

Ten years ago, I was a hardcore idealist. Folks were dying in cold, abandoned houses five minutes down the road while I was singing about Jesus in the cozy warmth of my living room. I lived in the "pill mill capital of the world", but I was completely blind to the needs of people who use drugs. Oh, I was certain I had the answer for them—for everyone really, regardless of their lot in life—but if one of these folks had walked into our church meeting off the street, I wouldn't have known what to do.

All of that changed when I caught a glimpse of Christ with a needle in his arm. Little by little, God took my hand and led me across a bridge spanning the chasm between idealism and reality. As we crossed that precipitous way, my uninformed prejudices about people who use drugs began to fade away like tree leaves in the fall. I took my seat at the feet of the marginalized and began to listen to their voice.

What I learned is that my lofty ideals are not what other people need from me. They don't need me pointing out their sins to them as if I don't do all the same things in my own more socially acceptable way. They don't need me telling them what to do and what not to do. They need someone who understands, or at least tries to understand, their struggle. They need a friend who will stand guard over their solitude, who will be there to support them if and when they decide it's time to change, and who will make provision for their health and safety in the meantime. If anything, they just need a gentle, faithful presence in their lives.

All they need is love. Nothing more and nothing less. Although I might add the caveat that love is generally more effective when it is properly educated. So with all your getting, get understanding, just like you're doing now by reading this book. Educated love is what people who use drugs need from you; why withhold it from them on account of your own personal ideals? Why not meet them where *they* are instead of requiring them to meet you where *you* are? Why not allow them the gift of their own experience—a gift that might call for different solutions than you can even now imagine?

Ok, sure. If you gave someone heroin, then I'll concede that you're enabling them to do something that might harm them. But not naloxone or fentanyl test strips. Don't just wash your hands of the matter, assuming there is nothing you can do to help before you've gotten all the facts. The only thing these harm reduction tools will enable people to do is stay healthy and alive.

And that's the whole point.

QUESTIONS FOR REFLECTION

Which of the two people in the opening story do you most relate to, the man who refused to give cash on principle or the woman who gave what she could with no questions asked? Have your feelings on the matter strengthened or softened after reading this chapter? Describe the evolution of your thought process.

_____

_____

_____

_____

_____

_____

_____

_____

_____

_____

_____

_____

_____

John Galsworthy said that our idealism increases in direct proportion to our distance from the problem. On a scale of 1 to 10, with 1 being very far and 10 being very close, where would you rate yourself in relation to the opioid overdose crisis? What steps can you take to gain a better understanding of the needs of people who use drugs?

_____

_____

_____

_____

_____

_____

_____

_____

_____

_____

_____

_____

In this chapter, we considered the dangers of illicit fentanyl and the value of fentanyl test strips. How is your mindset toward these and other harm reduction tools changing as you learn more about their practical uses?

_____

_____

_____

_____

_____

_____

_____

_____

_____

_____

_____

It has been said that no child grows up thinking that they want to become an addict one day. Most people who are caught in the throes of chaotic drug use arrived there due to a combination of debilitating factors, such as unresolved trauma, severe mental health challenges, or childhood abuse. Does this understanding help generate more compassion in you for people who use drugs? How can you further cultivate this mindset without allowing your own pain or compassion fatigue to cloud your judgment of people in need?

_____

_____

_____

_____

_____

_____

_____

_____

_____

_____

_____

SIX

HOW PRO-LIFE ARE YOU?

"For people of faith, harm reduction is a pro-life issue. You can't take seriously the words of Jesus in Matthew 25:40, that whatever you've done to the "least of" his brothers and sisters—in other words, the most vulnerable members of society—you've done also to him, and yet still argue that overdose victims should be left to die in the streets. It just doesn't work that way."

— *The Face of Addiction*

WORKING WITH MARGINALIZED PEOPLE has taught me three things.

First, you have to be a special kind of crazy to get involved in social work. Seriously, who wants to get their heart broken on a daily basis while working with the most vulnerable members of their community for a measly $40,000 a year? No, thanks.

The second lesson is that despite insanely low pay, long hours, and guaranteed heartache, social work, community organizing, and similar vocations are totally worth the investment. Crazy or not, there's nothing like the feeling you get when that guy you helped get his GED out of prison lands his first job and leaves the program because he no longer needs help supporting his family. Yes, please. I'll take some more of that.

But the third lesson is what I really want you to get. Attempting to walk in solidarity with marginalized individuals has taught me that we tend to lose compassion for people the older they get. It's like the more mistakes they make in life, the less we care to empathize with their plight. This is especially true for people who use drugs, and even more so if their drug use has gotten them entangled in the criminal justice system.

Think about it.

Perhaps you've seen how people rage against wrongdoing when they hear about a child who's been severely abused or neglected, as in some of the horror stories that routinely come out of the foster care system. This rage is totally understandable. But if you take time to really think it through, you probably also see the path that abused child is likely to take as they grow up into a traumatized adult. Sadly, you know that once they begin to project their pain onto other people, society won't be so kind and forgiving towards them then.

And the cycle of trauma repeats itself.

We fail to protect our children on the front end, then punish them for it on the back end. We're funny like that here in the West, and I don't mean funny in the "ha, ha" sense of the word. We reserve our rage for when kids grow up and become the perpetrator of suffering rather than just the victim. But the truth is we are *all* both victims and perpetrators of injustice. There seems to be no escaping this uncomfortable fact.

"But Josh, are you saying that adults shouldn't be held accountable for their actions? Even if their actions stem from unresolved trauma, aren't they still responsible for their choices? What about Hitler? We can't just let people do bad things and get away with it because they had a painful childhood."

Of course, I'm not saying that. Responsible adults should always be held accountable by society for anything they do to hurt other people. But if we want to break the cycle of unresolved trauma, we have to dig beneath the surface of behavioral issues for a better understanding of what it means to be human. Then we must allow this understanding to inform the way we approach each other at every age and level of society, including the person who uses drugs.

Speaking of Hitler, this is where I wanted to drop a fun little thought experiment on you involving time travel and the preventative murder of baby Adolf. Crazy, right? I wanted you to ponder whether you would kill an innocent child to save millions of lives whom that child might harm later in their life.

In my head, this experiment seemed like a brilliant idea, but I eventually decided against it. Most of our conversation here has been theologically and practically grounded, and it didn't seem right to switch gears by having you put on your philosopher's hat midway through the book.

The purpose, though, would have been to get you to admit that you believe in the sanctity of human life, even considering the horrible capacity that lies within each one of us to commit the most unspeakable atrocities. The next baby Hitler might be among us right now, after all, for as Aleksandr Solzhenitsyn famously said, "The line separating good and evil passes not through states, nor between classes, nor between political parties either—but right through every human heart."[1]

Knowing this, I'm betting you wouldn't kill someone just because they had the capacity to do evil. Nor would you end their life even on the likelihood that they might commit overtly wicked acts at some point down the road. I'm willing to bet this about you because you believe in the sanctity of human life, and that only God is qualified to sit in ultimate judgment over human beings. Your faith assures you that your role is simply to protect life in whatever form you find it, supporting its inherent capacity for good.

If I'm wrong in this wager, then forgive me for assuming the best of you. But I've spilled enough ink getting us to this point, so, for now, I'm going to stick with the assumption and carry on.

According to the most recent data, 128 people die from an accidental drug overdose every day in America.[2] The crisis is so severe that drug overdose is now the leading cause of accidental death in the United States, as nearly

1 million people have died of overdose since 1999.[3] If these numbers are hard to wrap your head around, then imagine that a Boeing 727 commercial airliner is going down in flames somewhere in America *every single day* with no survivors. That is exactly what is happening in our country.

Why should you, a person of faith, care about this tragedy? Because, as we've already established, you believe that all human life is precious and should be protected. You might even proudly refer to yourself as being "pro-life" based on this belief.

I just want to know one thing: how pro-life are you?

Don't worry, we're not about to wade into a debate about abortion. My only interest in raising this subject is to affirm your basic desire—again, assuming you possess it—to protect even the slightest possibility of human life. Even as I affirm the principle behind your desire to honor and protect human life, though, I also want to challenge your application of it.

Over 600,000 legal abortions were performed in the United States in 2018.[4] You probably care deeply about this fact. But do you also care that nearly 70,000 people died of an accidental overdose that same year, or that the total annual number of overdose deaths has risen by over 50% since that time?[5]

You do?

When was the last time you stood on the side of the street holding a sign about it, then? When was the last time you posted a witty meme on social media urging your friends to see people who use drugs as divine image bearers rather than human refuse? When was the last time you wrote to your state representative about the government's overwhelmingly poor response to the overdose crisis?

Of course, you might be thinking, *That's not a fair comparison because unborn babies are innocent. They haven't even been born, much less reached an age of accountability. Plus, babies are helpless; they can't defend or advocate for themselves. Drug addicts have made personal choices that hurt other people. They could help themselves if they really wanted to.*

But this line of thinking misses the forest for the trees, meaning that it fails to grasp the big picture by taking a limited view of the situation. Take a few steps back and you'll see that people who use drugs do, in fact, share one very important feature with unborn babies, and that is their *vast potential for good*. In addition to the basic value they possess as human beings, the possibilities underlying their lives are endless.

Who among us can say that that innocent-looking baby won't grow up to be the next Hitler, or that that person struggling toward recovery won't become a pastor and leader in their community one day? You honestly have no clue what course either of their lives will take despite your strongest assumptions, which is why you have no right to judge, condemn, or dismiss another person based on how they appear to you on any given day.

Consider the man to whom Jesus told the parable of the Good Samaritan. Seeking proof of his own righteousness, the man asked, "Who is my neighbor?" That is to say, who is worthy and deserving of my love? But Jesus flipped the script on him, turning the question around to ask, "Which of these people was a neighbor to the one in need?" In other words, it's not "who is your neighbor," but "who will *you* be a neighbor to?"

What was Jesus trying to do in that instance? The same thing I'm trying to do right now, which is to help you see the whole forest rather than just a few trees. I'm challenging you to enlarge the circle of your love, to widen the scope of your concern for the value of human life until it includes *everyone* at *all* points in their journey, including—yep, you guessed it—people who use drugs.

Correct me if I'm wrong, but the basic presumption of pro-life teaching is that all of life is a gift from God and that every human being is made in the divine image. This, at least, is the general thrust of both Jewish and Christian traditions. Furthermore, there is a clear prophetic thread woven throughout scripture that places special emphasis on God's unique relationship to those who are poor and outcast.

Shall I quote the Good Book to you?

Proverbs 14:31 says, "Those who oppress the poor insult their Maker, but helping the poor honors him." A little bit later, in chapter 19 verse 7, it says, "If you help the poor, you are lending to the Lord—and he will repay you!" Proverbs is chock-full of this sentiment. Then, of course, you can't forget Matthew 25, where Jesus goes so far as to self-identify with the most vulnerable members of his community, saying, "When you did it to one of the least of these my brothers and sisters, you were doing it to me!"

Here's the moral of the story: God cares deeply about those who have been relegated to the margins of society. In fact, according to Jesus, God cares about them so much that he will even *place himself in their shoes* and call his followers to serve him there, forever removing any loophole that his people might use to try to wriggle out of their social responsibility toward those who are in need.

Oh, come on now. Don't act like you haven't done it before.

At any rate, people who use drugs are made in the wondrous image of God. In the words of the Psalmist, they are "fearfully and wonderfully made."[6] If that truth bomb doesn't do it for you, then try this one on for size: for all intents and purposes, the guy on the street with the needle in his arm is Jesus. Jesus! There you go, try getting away from *that*.

It is this conviction, above all else, that provides the theological grounding for faith-based harm reduction.

Speaking of Jesus putting himself in the shoes of the outcast, I've got one more Bible story for you before we switch gears. In the opening passage of John 8, Jesus had one of his most profound encounters with the religious rulers in Jerusalem. Seriously, the first eleven verses of that chapter pack one heck of a punch.

It was early morning when Jesus arrived at the temple that day. As usual, people crowded around to hear him teach. But he hadn't gotten far into his discourse when a group of men showed up dressed to the hilt in long, flowing robes and religious phylacteries (look it up), dragging the bloodied body of a scantily clad woman.

Scandalous? You bet.

The men flung the woman to the ground at Jesus' feet, whereupon every eye in the crowd quickly fell. Some of the men carried stones. Quivering, the woman refused to look up, staring at the ground in front of her. A look of deep shame was etched on her features.

"Teacher," one of the Pharisees said, "this woman has been caught in the act of adultery."

Someone in the crowd stifled a gasp. Jesus said nothing.

"Now, in the Law," the man continued, "Moses commanded us to stone such women. So, what do you say?"

Jesus' disciples stood frozen just ten feet away. They had seen the religious rulers at Jerusalem try to trap their Master before, usually on some highly debated point of doctrine, but this time they seemed to have an airtight case from which Jesus surely could not escape. He would be forced to either uphold the Law or be discredited as a false teacher.

But when the disciples turned to look at Jesus, what they saw perplexed them.

Refusing to answer the Pharisee's question, Jesus stooped down next to the woman and began to write in the dirt with his finger. This bewildering act stunned the circle of men at first, but they soon regained composure and began to press the matter more intensely.

"Answer the question!" one shouted.

"The Law is clear," said another.

"Come on," prodded a nearby onlooker, "what are you waiting for?"

Finally, Jesus stood up. Deliberately, he looked into the eyes of the man who had first asked the question, and then at the others. As his gaze flowed from person to person, he said, "Let him who is without sin among you be the first to throw a stone at her."

Silence.

The only sound to be heard was the light brushing of Jesus' garment against his skin as he stooped down once more to resume writing in the dirt.

An eternity must have passed in that frightened woman's mind. One quiet minute turned into another, and another, and another, until at last—a sound.

The soft thump of a rock against the earth.

One by one, beginning with the oldest among them, the men quietly turned to walk away. The disciples looked on, still frozen. Finally, Jesus was left alone with the woman by his side. Standing up, he asked her, "Woman, where are they? Has no one condemned you?"

Finally grasping the courage to look him in the eye, she replied, "No one, Lord."

"Neither do I condemn you," Jesus said. "Go, and from now on sin no more."

First, notice what *doesn't* happen in this story. Jesus doesn't moralize about the woman's plight. He doesn't place conditions on his help. He doesn't even seem to care about the particulars of the accusations brought against her. He simply meets her at her point of need.

Next, notice what *does* happen. First of all, this was a display of sheer brilliance on Jesus' part. When faced with a clear binary choice—fidelity to the Law or mercy for the lawbreaker—Jesus answered in a way that turned the power of the Pharisees' accusation back upon themselves. With a few simple words, he effectively stripped the gavel from the hands of the saints while extending mercy to the poor sinner on whom their judgment was set to fall.

It's breathtaking, really, but what I most want you to see is the shocking beauty of Jesus' silent demonstration. Before he ever rises to answer her accusers, *Jesus places his own body down in the dirt with the woman.*

Full stop.

This incredible act of compassionate solidarity disrupted the expectations of everyone present on that day. Without the use of a single word, Jesus communicated unequivocally that the heart of God is to cut straight through bureaucratic red tape and meet people where they are with scandalous grace and radical love. Although the case against the woman seemed to be airtight when judged by the prevailing moral standard, Jesus found a way to protect and preserve her life, offering her redemption rather than condemnation.

Do I need to go on, or do you get the point? Surely you can see by now that the harvest of precious souls within the field of harm reduction is plentiful. But the number of laborers is so few. What are you waiting for, then? Maybe you've heard it said that being pro-life is all about protecting the unborn, but I'm telling you it's about protecting *all* human life from the womb to the tomb, regardless of whether you think they deserve it.

Believe it or not, my friend—your Lord is in the harm reduction business. Once you see this remarkable truth, the order of the day becomes simple. It is time to drop your stones, quit moralizing about the plight of people who use drugs, and follow him!

QUESTIONS FOR REFLECTION

Do you consider yourself to be pro-life? If so, do you possess a consistent ethic of human life that applies to every individual at *all* stages of human development? What does that look like for you?

_____

_____

_____

_____

_____

_____

_____

_____

_____

_____

What are some ways that churches and people of faith routinely "miss the forest for the trees" when it comes to serving the most vulnerable members of their community?

_____

_____

_____

_____

_____

_____

_____

_____

_____

_____

_____

If you could go back in time and kill baby Hitler, would you do it? Why or why not?

_____

_____

_____

_____

_____

_____

_____

_____

_____

_____

_____

Reflect on Jesus' encounter with the woman accused of adultery. Place yourself in the shoes of each party—disciples, Pharisees, onlookers, the woman herself—and describe the thoughts and feelings that arise in your heart as you witness Jesus' response.

_____

_____

_____

_____

_____

_____

_____

_____

_____

_____

_____

SEVEN

FROM THE OVERFLOW OF THE HEART

"I'm just a girl... I'm not an 'addict.' I'm not some piece of trash. I didn't choose to go through the things I went through. Who would?"

— **Christine, *The Face of Addiction***

WHEN WE SET OUT on this journey together, I promised to interrupt your thought patterns as gently as I possibly could. I'd like to think that was a very Christ-like gesture on my part, but I don't know. Reading scripture, it seems like Jesus wasn't afraid to ruffle feathers whenever he needed to make an important point.

Forget your typical Sunday school portrait of "lowly Jesus, meek and mild." Have you ever read Matthew 23? The man got practically livid when he saw religious people acting in ways that kept others from entering the kingdom of heaven, especially when they did it in the name of God.

"You shut the door of the Kingdom of Heaven in people's faces," he told one group of Pharisees. "You won't go in yourselves, and you don't let others enter either."[1]

In the same breath, he pointed out how they would travel over land and sea just to make a single convert. How is it that both these things could be true at the same time? And might the same paradox be true of many evangelical communities today, just in a different context? Are we all concerned about overseas missions work and "reaching the lost" on one hand while "shutting the door" to people in our own neighborhood on the other?

Back in the second chapter of this book, we looked at the story of the Canaanite woman who came to Jesus asking for help with her daughter. You might recall that Jesus behaved very curiously toward her in that encounter. First, he ignored her. Can you imagine that? The one who came to seek and save the lost, acting as if some poor woman didn't even exist.

Then, he referred to her as a "dog," which was a common Jewish epithet toward Canaanites. Did this callous disregard cause the most sensitive among his disciples to wince, or were they also prepared to turn her away, as they were in other instances?

The lady persisted, though, because she was desperate. Desperate people will do all kinds of bold things when they have nothing left to lose. And, at last, in response to her desperate act of trust, Jesus finally recognized her as a woman in need, lauding her faith in front of his disciples.

Canaanite people were stigmatized figures in Jewish eyes. They were looked down on as being "less than." Jesus' own disciples might have disparaged them for being *other* than the chosen people of God. This may have been the whole point behind Jesus' strange behavior. Perhaps he was acting in character as a common Jewish religious figure might, then leveraging the woman's response as a teaching moment—an object lesson in how to transcend cultural barriers and overcome social stigma that keeps people disconnected from God and one another.

You probably get where I'm going with this, but here's the point: similar to the Canaanite woman in Jesus' time, people who use drugs are stigmatized in our modern society. The correlation isn't one hundred percent, of course, but the principle is the same. And this stigmatization demonstrates itself in lots of ways, most of them quite subtle.

Starting with the way we talk.

Language matters because words possess power. I'm not talking about the "name-it-and-claim-it" mumbo jumbo that you hear from televangelists, but the inherent ability of human language to form perceptions that affect the way we relate to the world. Maybe you've never stopped to think about it, but this principle lies at the heart of Christian theology. Right at the bedrock, in the Creation story from the first chapter of Genesis, you can see it on full display.

Let's consider this for a moment. Maybe you're not aware, but there were multiple creation stories floating around the ancient near eastern world at the time of the writing of scripture. The Enuma Elish, for instance, was a Babylonian epic that many scholars believe the Jewish story was written to critique. You can look it up if you'd like.[2] I won't recount the whole story here, but let's just say the Babylonian gods Marduk and Tiamat got in one heck of a fight. When the dust settled after the last drop of blood had been spilled, the universe was allegedly born from their conflict.

Why is this comparison relevant to our discussion? Chiefly because of how the two stories differ. The Babylonian story, along with most other creation tales from the ancient near east, claimed that the universe was established out of bloodshed and conquest. The Babylonian writers, along with many others, would have us believe that violent battles between the gods are what ultimately led to the creation of the Earth and humanity.

Then along came the Jewish people making claims about God that were fundamentally different from those other stories. Instead of creating the world through violence and bloodshed, the Jewish writer/s insisted that God created everything through *the power of the spoken word*.

"And God said...and there was."[3]

No epic battles of divine conquest. No cutting the other gods in half. No taking power over one another. Just the proclamation of the divine Logos. Only the spoken Word of God.

This is huge.

The beauty of the Jewish story is found in how it portrays God being so full of creative energy that his heart poured forth with all manner of living things. Scripture shows the divine artist making something out of nothing, calling those things that were not as though they were and framing the universe through the power of the Word.[4]

The opening scene of the biblical narrative presents the germ of this idea: words have the power to form reality. However you choose to apply the idea (and it can be misapplied, as the money-grabbing preachers do), the principle is clear. Language matters because words have power.

Of course, you probably know the rest of the biblical creation story. At the end of the week, God created humanity in the divine image and likeness. That includes you, friend. You were dreamed up by God along with all the rest of us to be co-creators of our Father's world. That's the broader meaning behind God's instruction for Adam and Eve to "be fruitful, and multiply, and fill the earth," you know. God wasn't just telling his image-bearing co-creators to get busy in the bedroom but admonishing them to use the raw materials of creation to make all sorts of wonderful, beautiful things. It was a commission to continue the work that God had started, making visible the invisible content of their creative hearts.

What a calling!

Now then, enough about Babylonian gods, the divine logos, and other metaphysical mysteries of the faith. The question you care most about is what this means for you today, so let's turn toward application. Maybe you recall hearing the childhood jingle that "sticks and stones may break my bones, but words will never hurt me." Your momma might have told you this little ditty in a sincere attempt to help you feel better after the neighborhood bully called you a bad name. And heck, maybe it even worked. God bless your momma then, because she meant well. But wow, was she ever wrong.

Contrary to the common trope that words themselves do not cause harm, scripture tells us that the power of life and death is in the tongue. Those seemingly insignificant utterances that come out of your mouth a thousand times a day can either build people up or tear them down. The words you speak will either liberate or restrain.

And the point, which I've taken some time getting to, is that you would do well to remember this fact the next time you refer to someone as an addict. Or a junkie. Or a user. Or a—well, you get the point.

Maybe you've noticed that throughout this book I've been talking about people who use drugs in certain ways that avoid such common misnomers. You can be sure that this move was one hundred percent intentional. The only time I've used the language of "addicts" and "users" has been while utilizing what they call "speech-in-character." That is, when I've placed myself in the shoes of someone else and spoke like them. Otherwise, I've been careful to use *person-first language* when referring to people who use drugs.

Not addicts, but *people* who use drugs.

Not junkies, but *people* with a substance use disorder.

Not pill heads, but *people* who suffer with addiction.

People, people, people. We are talking about human beings here, after all. Remember, that guy with the needle in his arm is Jesus! He is a bearer of the divine image.

When it comes to human beings, certain descriptors can be helpful, especially in the early stages of identifying a problem. This is probably why so many people find it helpful to stand up in a support group meeting and introduce themselves as an alcoholic or an addict. They are simply being honest about their personal struggle, and honesty is always liberating.

The potential problem with any label, however, is twofold. First, if it's stigmatizing, that is obviously an issue. Second, even if it's accurate, it will always be too small to encompass the whole of an individual. Regardless of what you call me or who you know me as (such as a husband or a writer), I will always be far more than just that. This is true of anyone in any capacity, which is why it's important to be mindful of the language we use surrounding certain labels.

For instance, when I consider my friends who are in recovery, I will always respect their self-designation. One guy might refer to himself as an "addict," and I can see how this view might help him remember where he came from and stay humble as he seeks to leave his past behind. That's between him and his higher power.

At the same time, I won't ever refer to him as an addict myself because I know the tendency of society to see the label and miss the person. This is how all dehumanization starts, after all—with language. When you see an "addict," you subconsciously place limitations on that person based on your understanding of the category. But if you see a human being with a personal struggle that is not at all unlike your own (while being entirely unique to them at the same time), then you can approach them with compassionate understanding.

This is how you begin to help someone, by seeing them as a person with a name and not as a thing with a problem. Until you reach that point, all bets are off. We Christians have a hard time with this issue to begin with, as any Sunday morning service will show. We're all the time talking about "the lost," "the poor," "the world," "the unsaved," and so on. Evangelical theology makes it easy to see people in terms of a group designation rather than as individuals with unique needs that can only be understood in the context of a personal relationship.

Before we go on, let me tell you about my friend, Christine, whom I quoted at the beginning of this chapter. Christine was featured in chapter four of my first book, *The Face of Addiction*. She was such a beautiful soul. I say "was," sadly, because Christine died of an accidental drug overdose shortly before Christmas 2020. I lit a candle in her memory at a Naloxone Saves service (like the one I mentioned in Chapter 3) at an Episcopal church in southern Ohio whose members were just taking up the mantle of harm reduction ministry in the spring of 2021.

Christine's passion to end the stigma surrounding people who use drugs was contagious. She knew what she was talking about, too. She had about as rough a life as anyone I've known, and I should know, because in the months following my initial interview with her, I was helping her write her own book which detailed her personal history to an even greater extent.

When Christine sent me the Word doc and I began to read her story, I couldn't hold back my tears. Abuse, neglect, rape, abandonment, hopelessness - you name it, she lived it. But she found her way out of the darkness in the fall of 2017 after waking up to the sound of her son screaming her name over her apparently lifeless body. She had overdosed again, and he thought it was final.

Thankfully, it wasn't. I met her a year and a half later, after she had gone through treatment and entered recovery. At that point, she was hustling not to maintain her addiction but to raise awareness. She was rebuilding relationships within her family and creating a new meaning for her life by reaching out to other people who had experienced hardships similar to her own.

"I thought the bridges were burned completely," she told me. "My addiction kept telling me that it was too late, that I'd done too much. But it's never too late. After thirty-five years of addiction, even, it's never too late."

Christine found her way into a faith-based treatment center who worked with her and showed her that she was worth more than she had ever believed.

"I thought my life was over," she told me. "I figured that dying as a junkie was all I had to look forward to, but they stood beside me. They saw so much more in me than I had ever been told. They loved me until I could love myself."

The hope that Christine found in recovery motivated her to reach out to others. She wanted to open a safe house where people could stay while they were waiting to get into treatment. The last time I spoke to her, she was busy preparing meals for families in need over the holidays. But then, one month later, I received the shocking news that Christine had died. I didn't know any of her family or friends, but I tracked down her daughter on social media, who confirmed what I feared to be the case. Having relapsed, Christine felt too ashamed to reach out for help. The crushing weight of stigma was too much for her to bear. In a desperate bid to chase the pain away, she used too much, and no one was there to bring her back from the precipice before she slipped over the edge.

On the evening of May 17th, 2021, a candle burned on the altar of All Saints Episcopal Church in the presence of faithful witnesses. People of goodwill had gathered to honor the value of every human being regardless of their lot or their choices in life. Among them, in spirit, must surely have been the friend of Christine's who posted on her Facebook wall in the week following her death, wishing her peace and hoping that now she was, at last, in a more forgiving place.

You might say that I've written this entire book for Christine. Whenever I talk about harm reduction, this is why. Because Christine matters. As do all those whose lives have been lost to overdose and the war on drugs.

As a person of faith, you are poised to make a tremendous difference in this struggle. You have the potential to impact so many people and save multiple lives. So please, I beg you, for the love of God, and for the love of people like my friend, Christine, don't fail to heed this call. If you can't see the image of God in those who use drugs, then see the image of Christ, who offers himself as an object of faith and identifies with them in their suffering. Then, you will succeed in meeting them where they are and serving them at their point of deepest need.

Thinking back to when I interviewed Christine for my first book, I can't help but remember the way she turned the question about stigma back on me. "What will it take for others to see the value in people like me?" she asked, the urgency in her eyes speaking louder than the words. "I'm not an addict," she pleaded. "I'm just a girl!"

I'm just a girl. Not an addict. A girl. A human being.

In many ways, Christine's desperate plea to be known as something more than an addict was an echo of the Canaanite woman's desire to be recognized by Jesus. First, she was nobody. Then, a dog. And finally— "Dear *woman*," Jesus said to her, "your faith is great. Your request is granted."[5]

Lest you think I'm overreaching by using this story to highlight the power our words have to honor and restore those whom society has dehumanized, let's go back to Matthew 15 one more time. Just before Jesus met the Canaanite woman in the region of Tyre and Sidon, he was talking to a group of Pharisees who had come from Jerusalem specifically to contend with him about his disciples' failure to wash their hands before they ate.

Personal hygiene wasn't their concern, of course. Their contention had to do with the Jewish purity code. Ritual handwashing was an "age-old tradition" that signified a person's fidelity to the commands of God.

"Why do your disciples disobey this tradition?" they asked.

To which Jesus replied, as he often did, with a question of his own: "Why do you, by your traditions, violate the commandments of God?"

Using an example about the Sabbath to prove his point, Jesus cited the prophet Isaiah, who said of ancient Israel, "These people honor me with their lips, but their hearts are far from me."[6]

Then turning to the crowd, Jesus said, "Listen, and try to understand. It is not what goes into your mouth that defiles you; you are defiled by the words that come out of your mouth."

This startling assertion was such a direct affront to Jewish tradition that Jesus' own disciples quickly pulled him aside to make sure he knew just how much he had offended the Pharisees.

Oh, those guys?

"They are blind guides leading the blind," the Master replied, "and if one blind person guides another, they will both fall into a ditch."

Ouch. Alright, Lord, you've got our attention.

"Explain to us the parable that says people aren't defiled by what they eat," Peter said.

"Don't you understand yet?" Jesus asked. "Anything you eat passes through the stomach and then goes into the sewer. But the words you speak from the heart—that's what defiles you."

In other words (no pun intended), the way we talk reveals the attitude and condition of our hearts. If the words we speak are contentious, slanderous, and accusatory—well, then it's actually *we* who are defiled, not, as in this case involving the Pharisees and Jesus' disciples, the people we may be pretending to care about.

Those Pharisees had rolled into town, theological guns a-blazing, contending that Jesus' disciples had defiled themselves by what they put into their mouths with unwashed hands. But Jesus inverted their logic, claiming, in effect, that it was actually the Pharisees who were unclean, as evidenced by the accusatory words coming out of their mouths.

Are you sitting down? Because I'm about to suggest a very powerful correlation between this story and our conversation about people who use drugs. If it stings a little, just remember that I believe in your ability to receive it; otherwise, I wouldn't have gone to so much trouble setting it up.

Here goes.

Most of the stigma surrounding people who use drugs comes from those who believe that they occupy a moral high ground over anyone who would snort a line of cocaine or inject heroin into their veins. Whether such folks admit it or not, they look down on people who use drugs as if those people are somehow unclean—immoral, weak-willed, unrighteous, and so on—because of the substances they choose to consume.

If you don't believe me, then why do they say a person is "dirty" when they are actively using drugs, and "clean" when they abstain?

From the abundance of the heart, the mouth speaks.

But I need to tell you something, and just like Jesus admonished the crowd that day in Galilee, I need you to try to understand. It is not what goes into a person but what comes out that truly defiles them.

Let's say it one more time for good measure: It is not what goes into a person that defiles them, but what comes out of their heart, *as evidenced by the words they speak.*

So, it's not so much the man on the street with an unsterilized needle in his arm who is defiling himself, but the person in the pew at the church down the road whose words about that man, whether spoken in public or private, betray the stigma they carry in their heart toward him. Speaking about another person as though they were something other or less than the beloved child of God that they are—doing violence to the image of God with stigmatizing, dehumanizing language—*that* defiles a person far more than shooting up with a dirty needle.

If this chapter was an ancient psalm, here would be the point at which the Psalmist would remark, "Selah." Although the exact meaning of this ancient Hebrew word is unknown, many scholars and commentators believe it was intended as a break in the message, encouraging the reader to pause and reflect on what they had just heard.

So, Selah.

Pause for a bit and think about what I've said here. Take a long, hard look in the mirror that I've held up for you. Consider the possibility that the way you talk about people who use drugs might be contributing to their harm. Because if your language reinforces the popular cultural narrative, then yeah, it probably is hurting them. I'm not asking you to beat yourself up about it, just to be more mindful of the impact your words can have on other people.

At the end of the day, we all have room to grow. Stigma is deadly, though, so this chapter had to be written. The power of life and death is in your tongue. Use it wisely.

QUESTIONS FOR REFLECTION

Having considered the potential impact of stigmatizing language, what specific words from your vocabulary might you reconsider using when it comes to people who use drugs?

_____

_____

_____

_____

_____

_____

_____

_____

_____

_____

_____

_____

Can you think of a time in your life when another person used stigmatizing language toward you? What assumptions did this other person hold that led them to regard you in this way? How did it impact you?

_____

_____

_____

_____

_____

_____

_____

_____

_____

_____

_____

_____

What other ways could the story of the Canaanite woman be used to compare how people who use drugs are viewed by society today?

_____

_____

_____

_____

_____

_____

_____

_____

_____

_____

_____

_____

Reflecting on Christine, whose passion for recovery was not enough to overcome the shame she felt after relapsing, what do you think it would take for someone like her to feel comfortable, accepted, and safe enough to come forward and ask for help? Does your church or faith community provide that kind of environment?

_____

_____

_____

_____

_____

_____

_____

_____

_____

_____

_____

EIGHT

BLESSED ARE THE PEACEMAKERS

"A true revolution of values will soon cause us to question the fairness and justice of many of our past and present policies. On the one hand we are called to play the Good Samaritan on life's roadside, but that will be only an initial act. One day we must come to see that the whole Jericho Road must be transformed so that men and women will not be constantly beaten and robbed as they make their journey on life's highway. True compassion is more than flinging a coin to a beggar. It comes to see that an edifice which produces beggars needs restructuring."

— **Martin Luther King, Jr.**[1]

So, WE'RE BEGINNING TO near the end of our journey together. Kudos to you for sticking it out this far. We've only got three more chapters, a brief conclusion, and an appendix to go. In the last chapter, we're going to review a set of practical suggestions on how you can get involved in harm reduction work, whether as an individual, a small group, or a faith community.

Before we arrive at our destination, however, I think it's only fair to warn you that we've got one more crazy turn to take along the way. In fact, now is probably a good time to tighten your seatbelt. I don't want you flying out the window on me before we get where we're going. I would let you close your eyes, but then you wouldn't be able to read the book!

Consider this your content warning. If you don't like what I'm getting ready to say—well, at least I warned you. Having come this far together, though, I'm confident that you're ready to do some heavy lifting.

By now, you've seen that harm reduction is a set of principles and practices aimed at mitigating the harms associated with drug use. When viewed in this light, the overdose crisis is rightly framed as a public health issue.

At the same time, the overdose crisis is more than just a public health concern. Activists are not only trying to reduce potential harms associated with drug use, but also to address issues stemming from our country's inhumane drug *laws*. When viewed in this light, harm reduction is better understood as a movement for social justice.

And when given the proper theological framework, we might even be so bold as to say that harm reduction is a ***social justice movement fueled by radical love***.

In America, this holy work first began in the streets among people who were at risk of dying in the HIV epidemic of the 1980s. Community organizers and activists began distributing clean syringes beneath the radar of law enforcement long before the medical profession got on board, doing whatever they could with whatever means they had to save the lives of their friends, family, and neighbors. By the time public health experts caught on to the need for radical life-saving measures that went above and beyond what the legal system would allow, the AIDS crisis was nearing its peak. The task of harm reduction, however, had just begun. For a brief overview of this important history, check out the appendix at the end of this book.

Working in my own community, I've noticed the tension that still exists between public health institutions and law enforcement officials. In fact, in all the recovery-based coalition meetings and workshops I regularly attend, rarely does anyone have the nerve to address the elephant in the room—America's need for criminal justice reform.

And by reform, I mean a complete overhaul of the system as it currently exists.

Sure, you might occasionally hear someone talk about partnering with law enforcement to help reduce recidivism rates. That's all fine and good as far as it goes, especially as long as the current system stands, but there are bigger questions that need to be asked.

For instance, anyone in the helping professions can tell you about the need for more funding in social services. Advocates could go on for hours about how hard it is to find sustainable revenue streams to support programs that care for the most vulnerable members of our population. This is a perpetual challenge that all harm reductionists and public health workers face. But there is one field where all kinds of money is being spent to tackle the problem of drug use, and with overwhelmingly poor outcomes.

That would be the criminal justice system.

Now, go down to your local courthouse and volunteer for grand jury duty. Sit in that chair for a couple months and watch as your county prosecutor parades case after case before you and your peers involving nothing more than simple drug possession. Such charges make up most criminal cases in rural America. I shudder to think of all the hard-earned tax money that is being spent every day on indictments, lab tests, prosecuting fees, and other costs related to the never-ending war on drugs. In 2015, the Drug Policy Alliance estimated that the United States spends $51 billion annually on drug war initiatives; other sources estimate that the U.S. has spent a cumulative $1 trillion dollars as of 2021.[2]

"But Josh, are you saying that crimes associated with substance use, such as theft, domestic violence, and operating a vehicle while under the influence, shouldn't be held accountable?"

Of course not. Any and all criminal activity that involves one person harming another should be held accountable, no matter what leads to it. But what happens when the harms perpetrated on vulnerable people are a direct result of drug law enforcement? Who should be held accountable then?

The War on Drugs officially began on June 18, 1971, when President Nixon declared drug use to be "public enemy number one" in America. "In order to fight and defeat this enemy," he said, "it is necessary to wage a new, all-out offensive."[3] So began the nation's decades-long climb toward mass incarceration. At its peak in 2009, over 1.6 million people were imprisoned across the country. Today, the United States, despite making up only 5% of the global population, is home to more than 20% of the world's incarcerated population.

So much for "land of the free."

Although the drug war didn't gain official credence until the Nixon administration, the U.S. government had long been using drug laws to target specific minority communities, such as Chinese immigrants in the 1870's and Mexican migrants in the 1910's and 1920's. In a now infamous 1994 interview that was only published in 2016, John Ehrlichman, a top Nixon aide, admitted that the administration's new offensive was intentionally designed to target black people and anti-war "hippies." The long, checkered history of America's drug war has been documented by Johann Hari's groundbreaking book, *Chasing the Scream*.

So, there are a plethora of good reasons why we need to end the war on drugs, but recognizing them will require you to think deeper than the popular narrative underlying America's "tough on crime" approach to drug use.

Let's start with the fact that people are always going to use drugs whether or not it is legal to do so. As the historian Will Durant pointed out, no civilization in human history has survived without the help of stimulants and narcotics.[4] The difference between brewing poppy seed tea and injecting fentanyl, however, cannot be understated. The stakes are higher now than they were even a hundred years ago because the chemical compounds being sold on the streets today are far more dangerous than the simple substances of the past on which today's analogues are based. For this reason alone, it is vital that we turn to the creation of a well-regulated, safe supply of drugs.

The drug war, however, is based on prohibitionist ideals—namely, the notion that all recreational drug use is morally wrong and should be discouraged by threat of force, state-sanctioned violence, and criminal punishment. For all intents and purposes, though, it is prohibition that kills. Just like the criminalization of alcohol in the early 20th century, current drug laws result in the rise of cartels and black markets, gang violence, the unregulated manufacture of dangerous chemical substances, and the unnecessary incarceration of nonviolent individuals whose lives are consequently destroyed by their involvement in the criminal justice system.

All this even though most people who use drugs do not commit violent crimes. How much more would it help those who do have a substance use disorder to fund harm reduction services and evidence-based treatment programs rather than pumping endless dollars into a criminal justice system whose best outcomes are found in programs (such as drug courts) that represent a general departure from the conventional approach?

In either case, the creation of a safe drug supply would at least keep people from dying. As you recall, it is the presence of fentanyl in the illicit drug supply that is behind our skyrocketing rates of accidental overdose. And it is prohibition that unwittingly encourages the unregulated manufacture and distribution of increasingly dangerous chemical compounds. I really don't know how else to say it. The sharp rise in accidental overdose deaths due to synthetic opioids manufactured by rogue chemists in clandestine labs is a direct result of the war on drugs. When law enforcement shuts down one source of supply, another source will spring up to take its place. Only then the market is driven deeper underground, where there will inevitably be fewer safety regulations and greater potential for harm.[5]

Do you want to help people? Do you want to save lives? Then you've got to re-evaluate your understanding of drug use and addiction. Conventional thinking simply will not do. We've got to revolutionize our approach to both the problem and the solution. People are dying of accidental overdose in record numbers precisely *because* of the war on drugs, not in spite of it.

This idea might sound very strange to you, and if so, that's ok. It sounded strange to me the first time I heard it, too. But think the matter through. Read and research the issue for yourself. Most of all, listen to people with lived experience. Eventually, you'll see that we must address this crisis at its root.

Harm reduction may begin among compassionate individuals and grass-roots organizations, but to be truly effective, it will have to find acceptance among legislators at the state and federal level. Even the most radical interventions, such as the state of Rhode Island's recent legalization of safe-injection sites, when isolated from wider social policies, will struggle to make more than a marginal impact on the overall number of overdose deaths due to the sheer volume of the problem.[6]

Simply put, we have to do more. Although safe injection sites are a welcome addition to the harm reduction movement that will undoubtedly save lives, it would take literally thousands of them spread out across the country to reach all the people who are in need. Such a tremendous financial investment by state and local governments may be a necessary step for now given how slowly the wheels of change grind, but it begs the question of our legislators: why not just go all the way?

Back in chapter four, we applied Jesus' parable of the Good Samaritan to the mission of harm reduction. That was for you, the individual, and your local faith community. Here, we're stepping back and taking a wider view of the problem. For as Martin Luther King, Jr. said, playing the Good Samaritan on life's roadside is only an initial act. Ultimately, "we must come to see that the whole Jericho Road must be transformed so that men and women will not be constantly beaten and robbed as they make their journey on life's highway." Echoing this principle, Desmond Tutu remarked, "There comes a point when we need to stop just pulling people out of the river. We need to go upstream and find out why they are falling in."

Consider these additional disruptive thoughts.

Most people who use substances do *not* become dependent on their use. Furthermore, the majority of those who develop substance use disorders do so early in life. Assuming they survive the harms associated with both their drug use and the drug war, many of those folks will naturally grow out of their addictions over time. Maybe not all, but many.[7]

These simple facts strongly suggest that we should focus more on a person's *relationship* to substances than the substances themselves (present conversation about the dangers of illicit fentanyl notwithstanding), because therein lies the risk of chaotic drug use. As author Maia Salavitz points out in her book, *Unbroken Brain: A Revolutionary New Way of Understanding Addiction*, addiction is best conceived of as a developmental learning disorder rather than a chronic brain disease. This innovative concept has the potential to guide us away from the criminal justice approach to a wide scale model of harm reduction. The main barrier standing in the way of this redirection is misinformed prejudice.

This is a bit of a soapbox for me, but as far as I can tell, the common belief that substances are addictive in and of themselves is somewhat of a myth. Chemical dependency and physical withdrawal symptoms may be real, but most people who use drugs do not become psychologically "addicted" to them in the way we typically understand addiction.

Are certain substances dangerous? Yes. Do many people habitually use drugs as an unhealthy coping mechanism? Yes. Can the unbridled use of psychoactive substances harm or even destroy your life? Absolutely. But will you get "hooked" on marijuana just because you smoked it one time and got high? Chances are, probably not—especially later in life when your brain is no longer in its early developmental stages.

So, when I suggest that the myth of the demon drug is just that—a myth—I'm saying that people aren't chasing the substance so much as they're chasing a feeling of pleasure or escape from pain that they have learned to associate with its use. This means that we're missing the mark by focusing on substance use itself as the problem, a distinction that must not be overlooked in regard to both treatment and prevention.

So yes, the presence of fentanyl in the illicit drug supply is the main driver behind the overdose crisis, and the proliferation of fentanyl is a direct result of the war on drugs. But as economists Anne Case and Angus Deaton show in their book, *Deaths of Despair and the Future of Capitalism*, the primary determinants of the addiction epidemic plaguing western society are social. Drugs are not the problem. Poverty, educational disparities, and unaffordable health care are the problem. Our failure to provide for healthy childhood development is the problem. The social dislocation of individuals who cannot maintain the frantic pace of western society is the problem. And yes, the drug war itself is part of the problem. To stem the tide of the overdose crisis, we have to lay the ax at the root of the problem, rather than hacking mindlessly at the branches.

As difficult as this effort may be, bringing more nuance to the public conversation surrounding drug use will be required to convince legislators of the changes we need to make in our social policies. As it currently stands, few of them are willing to go against the grain of the traditional American drug war mentality. Why are they unwilling? Two reasons mainly, the first being money. Fighting drug-related crime is a lucrative business, after all, one big, perpetual revenue stream. The second reason, which I have focused on more intently throughout this book, is moral ideology.

Let's say a few more words about that.

The overdose crisis could be solved by decriminalizing drug possession and creating a safe drug supply. Contrary to popular fears, such a radical shift in policy wouldn't result in everyone suddenly deciding to spend the rest of their lives high on drugs. It would, however, save countless lives.

Just think of it! Millions of dollars could be redirected toward social services, education, and truly effective means of prevention. In the meantime, people would stop dying from illicit substances tainted with fentanyl and other dangerous chemical compounds. Drug-related crime would decrease as gangs and cartels were forced out of business. The entire culture would begin to transform.

Our elected officials won't do this, though—not without a fight—because aside from the money issue, they are captive to a moral ideology that says, "drugs are bad." Therefore, they don't have the courage to risk coming off as "soft on crime" or as encouraging drug use. Never mind that no one views the sale of alcohol this way because, for some reason, that's different (except it's not, because the misuse of alcohol does more long-term damage to the human body than any other substance currently in use). The only difference lies in our entirely arbitrary cultural acceptance of one substance over the other.

The moral of the story is simple: prohibition does far more harm than good. All the naloxone in the world won't save as many lives as a safe drug supply would. To provide for the health and safety of people who use drugs, our overarching priority must be to abolish the war on drugs, because the war on drugs is really a war on people who use drugs. Maybe you've heard it said that we have to be tough on crime to solve the problem of drug use and addiction, but I'm telling you that the only way to win the war on drugs is to end it.

It's frustrating to hear the militant, impersonal language of the drug war used to describe the crisis our society is facing. Imagine the shift in public consciousness if radio announcers, journalists, TV anchors, and legislators talked about finding ways to heal and care for our neighbors instead of "combating the opioid epidemic." We Americans are so obsessed with war that we frame almost everything in relation to it, whether it be drugs, terror, or even poverty.

Equally amazing is the way society criminalizes some forms of addiction while encouraging others. Those of us with addictions that are socially acceptable (coffee, anyone?) tend to look down on those whose addictions have been stigmatized, but, at the end of the day, we're not that different. We enjoy our lives of comfortable hypocrisy, though, so we refuse to acknowledge this fact while our less fortunate neighbors suffer needlessly under the weight of "criminal justice."

Ultimately, addiction is a bio-psycho-social issue that requires compassionate care to adequately address, and criminal justice plays very little part in this process.[8] The threat of punishment might scare a few people straight, so to speak, but it will never heal the brokenness and pain in their souls. And until you've gone there, you've done nothing to address the problem of addiction. Isn't this what people of faith are supposed to be all about?

In Jesus' iconic Sermon on the Mount, he said, "Blessed are the peacemakers, for they will be called the children of God."[9] Many Christians regard this statement in a metaphysical way that has little relevance to everyday life. A few radical souls will apply it to physical warfare, and fewer still will apply to the inherently violent ways we talk about and relate to our fellow human beings on a day-to-day basis.

All of which I would encourage you to do, of course, but to my knowledge, no one has yet applied Jesus' call to peacemaking to the global war on drugs. Although signs of its impending collapse are appearing on the horizon, there is still so much work to be done to dismantle the systemic injustices of this war. Life-saving work that will impact the most vulnerable members of our communities—those whom Jesus expressly identifies himself with—for good.

You can be a vital part of the harm reduction movement, my friend. And you should be, for you possess a deep, rich well of faith from which to draw courage and inspiration for the work. You've heard the Spirit's call to follow Christ as he tears down walls of hostility between mortal enemies. You've tasted a peace that passes understanding, and you long to share that peace with others. Now, you have the theological framework necessary to engage in a ministry that has been too long neglected by the faith community.

As harm reductionist Blyth Barnow has said, "We know that naloxone saves, but that is not enough. To end overdose, we must end the war on drugs." And all the people said, "Amen!"

QUESTIONS FOR REFLECTION

Of all the disruptive ideas contained in this chapter, which one is the hardest for you to hear? What do you fear the most when considering these thoughts?

_____

_____

_____

_____

_____

_____

_____

_____

_____

_____

_____

_____

How does it feel to learn that drug laws have been used to selectively target minority groups throughout America history?

_____

_____

_____

_____

_____

_____

_____

_____

_____

_____

_____

It's been said that the definition of insanity is doing the same thing over and over again and expecting different results each time. With this idea in mind, why do you think legislators and law enforcement officials continue to spend so much time, money, and energy waging a war on drugs when that war has been proven ineffective?

_____

_____

_____

_____

_____

_____

_____

_____

_____

_____

_____

Reflect on the quote by Martin Luther King, Jr. that was shared in this chapter, particularly the last line: "True compassion is more than flinging a coin to a beggar. It comes to see that an edifice which produces beggars needs restructuring."

_____

_____

_____

_____

_____

_____

_____

_____

_____

_____

_____

NINE

A PARABLE INSPIRED BY A PANDEMIC

THE YEAR 2020 WILL go down in history for many reasons, some less tragic than others. Those of us who lived through the early days of the COVID-19 pandemic in the United States, for instance, will always remember the great toilet paper shortage of that fateful spring (I still blame the media for that one). Then there was *Tiger King*, that incredible Netflix debacle that kept millions of us entertained amidst the uncertainty of society's initial lockdowns. And Zoom—don't even get me started on all those awkward online meetings. To be honest, my family never really mastered the whole remote learning thing.

None of these lighthearted memories are meant to diminish the pain experienced by so many people during those years, of course. On the contrary, while I believe in the power of laughter to bring comfort in times of distress, I think it's important that we never turn our attention away from the suffering that surrounds us. This conviction is what compels me to point out that the opioid overdose crisis has not gone away despite the media's more recent focus on the coronavirus pandemic.

In fact, not only is the crisis continuing, but it's getting worse. Far worse. Under the shadow of COVID-19's ominous spread, the United States saw a *30% increase* in accidental overdose deaths in 2020.[1] In November 2021, the CDC released provisional data indicating an estimated 100,306 drug overdose deaths in the United States during a 12-month period ending in

April 2021. In case you're wondering, yes, that staggering figure is absolutely a new record. According to NPR's Brian Mann, if current trends continue (as of the time of this writing, at least), drug overdose will soon kill more people every day than the coronavirus itself.[2]

About midway through the first year of the pandemic, it occurred to me that the advent of COVID-19 represented an apocalyptic moment for western civilization. Not in the *Left Behind*, end-of-the-world sense that you're probably familiar with, but in the way it presented an opportunity for us to reimagine the way we do life together as a society. More specifically, I've come to believe that the "lockdown" experience we were all forced to endure held many important lessons related to mental health, substance use, and incarceration as a response to addiction.

My thoughts on this matter coalesced one day into a Facebook post. I'd like to share that post with you now as a bridge between our conversation in the last chapter about the drug war and the case study we're going to look at next. Having said this much just to provide historical context for future readers who didn't get the pleasure of watching *Tiger King*'s Netflix debut, I offer it to you here without interpretation as a kind of parable inspired by a pandemic.

· · · ● · ● · ● · ·

Them (prior to the pandemic): "Drugs are bad! We need to lock people up so they'll stop using them!"

Me: "But research shows that incarceration does more harm than good to people with a substance use disorder."

Them: "That's just liberal snowflake nonsense! People won't get help unless we force them to!"

Me: "So, you're saying that the solution to addiction is social isolation, and we should take away the rights and freedoms of people who use drugs to help them see the light?"

Them: "Yes, absolutely, if that's what it takes! If they can't find rock bottom on their own, we'll help 'em out a little. We gotta use the carrot *and* the stick, baby."

Me: "Hmm..."

(One year later)

Them (after lockdown, amidst quarantine): "Did you see the latest statistics? It's awful how many people are dying from accidental overdose!"

Me: "Yeah, the presence of fentanyl in the drug supply is getting worse due to the black market created by the war on drugs—"

Them: "I bet it's the pandemic."

Me: "Oh, really?"

Them, nodding their head definitively: "Yep. All this social isolation and restricted mobility isn't good for folks with an addiction. They need to be connected with other people or else their mental health will just get worse!"

Me: "So, let me get this straight. You're saying that the solution to addiction is social connection, and we should maintain the rights and freedoms of people who use drugs so they are less likely to overdose and die?"

Them: "Exactly! Isn't it obvious?"

Me: "Yeah, I guess it is."

QUESTIONS FOR REFLECTION

How does it impact you to know that accidental drug overdose is now the leading cause of death for people over 50 years of age in America?

_____

_____

_____

_____

_____

_____

_____

_____

_____

_____

Do you recall hearing the argument made during the COVID pandemic that social isolation was not good for people with mental health and addiction issues? Have you ever considered the correlation between the effects of the lockdown and our normal practice of incarcerating people who use drugs? What significance do you see here?

_____

_____

_____

_____

_____

_____

_____

_____

_____

_____

_____

Ten

A TALE OF TWO CITIES

"I remember my dad telling me when I was younger, 'Love people through hard things.' That's the whole idea behind agape-love. It's unending. There's no other way; people just end up alone. And if you're alone, you don't get anything. You don't get anything done. We're meant to be in community. We're meant to take care of each other."

— **Brooke Parker**

IN CHAPTER EIGHT, I made some bold statements about the harmful effects of the drug war, such as "prohibition kills' (try putting that one on a t-shirt). Since this is such an important part of our conversation, and because it will serve you better to provide concrete examples to back up these statements, let's end with two relevant case studies from rural America.

Case study #1 - SOAR (Solutions Oriented Addiction Response) in Charleston, WV

The first study comes from the city of Charleston in the heart of Kanawha County, West Virginia. Described by residents as a "capitol city with small town charm," Charleston sits at the convergence of the Elk River and the

Kanawha River in the Appalachian Mountains. According to Mayor Amy Shuler Goodwin, the people of Charleston are known for their genuine hospitality.[1] Like most cities, however, hospitality is harder to come by for people at the margins.

In the spring of 2021, Kanawha County was carrying the torch, as it had for many years, of having the nation's highest rates of drug addiction and overdose death. On top of this dubious honor, the city of Charleston was buckling under the surge of a related public health emergency, what CDC officials were calling the "most concerning" HIV outbreak in recent history.[2]

To shed some light on that statement, consider these statistics. In 2014, only 12% of HIV cases in West Virginia were the result of IV drug use. By 2019, however, that figure had risen to 64%. Kanawha County had only two cases in 2018, but that number grew to 15 in 2019 and at least 35 in 2020.[3] What accounted for the surge? Multiple factors, no doubt. But one very significant catalyst can be traced to 2018, when the Kanawha County Health Department's syringe service program (SSP) was shut down due to mounting political pressure.

Syringe service programs are better known to most people as "needle exchanges." SSPs are community-based intervention programs that provide a range of harm reduction services including, but not limited to, vaccinations, STD testing, linkage to care for infectious diseases and substance use disorder treatment, and access to sterile syringes.

SSPs are nothing new at this point in history. Decades of research have demonstrated their ability to improve public health and safety. Consequently, SSPs are recommended by the CDC as a best practice for preventing disease outbreaks among intravenous drug users. Although not undisputed (as you'll see here in a minute), this lesson has been clear since the initial HIV epidemic of the 1980s. For more information on the public health impact of early syringe exchange programs, check out the appendix at the back of this book.

So, why did the Kanawha County Health Department close their SSP in 2018? Because certain residents and community stakeholders, including some within the mayor's office, claimed that the exchange was nothing more than a "cattle call for junkies." Although there was nothing illegal about its operation, and the city had no ordinance on the books restricting its use, the department decided to close up shop in response to the demands placed upon them by social stigma and political pressure.

In the wake of this devastating loss, other concerned citizens stepped in to fill the void. Groups like SOAR (Solutions Oriented Addiction Response), an all-volunteer grassroots harm reduction organization based in Charleston, and individuals like Brooke Parker, who serves as SOAR's vice president. They launched a makeshift syringe exchange in parking lots on Charleston's west side during the early days of the COVID-19 pandemic. Local police attempted to chase them away, but they found refuge at a nearby church. Setting up for only two hours at a time, SOAR witnessed *300 people* come through the exchange each week due to word-of-mouth advertising alone.

Reporting on SOAR's intervention efforts in December 2020, the Mountain State Spotlight quoted one of their program participants as saying, "People can't get needles. I've watched them dig used ones out of the dirt and inject because they're that desperate. I've seen needles break in people's arms."[4] After receiving her HIV test results, the woman gathered her things to leave, thanking SOAR's team members for saving her life once again.

"This is what happens when public health fails," Parker says. "Communities step up, especially here in Appalachia, because we know that nobody is coming to save us. We take care of our own."

Unfortunately, every public health organization that serves people who use drugs is forced to do so under the shadow of the criminal justice system. The only needle drop box in Charleston is located in front of the Health Department, where a police car routinely parks outside. This shadow led one of SOAR's clients to declare that she would rather "die in the street" than visit her local health department.

If this much pressure surrounds state-sanctioned institutions like public health departments, can you imagine the challenges being faced by community-based harm reduction programs operating on a shoestring budget with volunteer labor?

How about a six-month long criminal investigation, for starters? Because that's exactly what happened to SOAR in the winter of 2020. Backed by city council, Charleston police ramped up their hostilities toward SOAR's activities. Parker herself has been screamed at and harassed by law enforcement officials. Certain officers are known to dump confiscated "works" (clean syringes and other drug-related paraphernalia meant to protect the health of SOAR's participants) into the river. After dumping the box, officers will take pictures of the alleged "syringe litter," sometimes placing the materials around the body of an overdose victim to make it look like they found the person laying on a pile of needles. Drug War propaganda at its finest.

In March 2021, the West Virginia Senate passed SB 334, regulating syringe service programs by requiring licenses for syringe collection and distribution programs. Under this bill, operators would be required to offer an array of health outreach services, including overdose prevention education and substance abuse treatment program referrals.[5] According to the legislation, such programs could only operate with the joint approval of a sheriff and the county commission. This move effectively placed public health in the hands of local law enforcement officials, many of whom believe that SSPs only result in more abandoned needles being left in public spaces, despite all evidence to the contrary.

Charleston city council initiated a congressional inquiry, prompting a visit from the CDC in the spring of 2021. While federal representatives affirmed the importance of harm reduction, local officials remained unphased. One councilperson went so far as to ask the CDC representative "how much they were paid" to give a false report about the situation in Charleston.[6] With similar pomp, the state senator who sponsored SB 334 laughingly claimed that the city was going to show the CDC a thing or two about handling an

HIV outbreak. After a legal battle was waged by the ACLU (American Civil Liberties Union) alleging the unconstitutionality of SB 334, a federal judge ruled in July 2021 that the measure was indeed enforceable, requiring SOAR to either halt its needle exchange program or go underground.[7]

"Charleston is West Virginia's capitol, so every city and town in the state looks to us for direction," Parker says in a personal letter. "The passing of SB 334 in 2021 made low-barrier harm reduction illegal across the state. We set the standard."

During the criminal investigation, only one other harm reduction program stayed open in Charleston. According to its website, West Virginia Health Right's mission is to "provide comprehensive quality healthcare to impoverished uninsured/underinsured adults regardless of insurance or financial status."[8] That may sound nice, but many community members claim that the organization's practices are too restrictive for people who need their help the most. Personal ID is required to receive services, and some participants have been kicked out of the program after making just one mistake. Health Right also tracks all of the needles it distributes, citing personal responsibility as a basis for the practice. While needle-tracking might seem like a common-sense measure on the surface, it often deters vulnerable people from using the service because they're afraid that the tracking is part of a sting operation which will land them in jail.

"West Virginia Health Right and Charleston city council both lean heavily on the value of personal accountability, believing they are responsible to the wider community to not enable drug use by conducting what they call 'free needle giveaways'," Parker says. "SB 334 is modeled directly after their program. But I've lost track of how many individuals have fallen through the cracks trying to keep up with all the restrictions and barriers they place on life-saving services. When people found out we didn't have any needles, they were literally sobbing in the street. We were reduced to handing out zip lock baggies of bleach to at least offer them something to help."

In case you're wondering how a bag of bleach can save someone's life, you might be interested to learn the history of harm reduction in America. Handing out bleach baggies was a primitive intervention practiced by early harm reductionists in places like Chicago and New York City in the 1980's. Check out Maia Salavitz's book, *Undoing Drugs: The Untold Story of Harm Reduction and the Future of Addiction*, for a deeper dive into this story.

Most of SOAR's clients are 25-35 years old (few live beyond 40), and nearly all of them fall well beneath the poverty line. Many individuals are unhoused and face severe mental health challenges, including substance use disorders.[9] Their struggles stem from the fallout of generational poverty and other complex personal and social issues. This complexity, Parker explains, is why it's so important for people to have access to harm reduction services.

Dr. Sally Hodder, a West Virginia University infectious disease expert, agrees: "In places such as West Virginia, where the collapse of the coal mining industry and extreme poverty have exacerbated the opioid epidemic, de-criminalizing substance abuse, providing clean, safe places for syringe service programs and other interventions, and offering comprehensive HIV prevention, care, and treatment services are all essential to ending these intertwined epidemics."[10]

In other words, the ultimate solution to Charleston's public health crisis surrounding drug use and addiction is to end the war on drugs. Harms stemming from the drug war are compounding in ways that may seem trivial when viewed from the suburbs, but to marginalized individuals who are struggling just to survive, they are devastating. When asked to explain what is driving the public stigma against people who use drugs, Parker points to "value-driven judgments." She believes that conservative ideology about drug use is keeping the most vulnerable members of her community from getting the help they need to stay alive.

"Privilege protects itself," she boldly asserts, meaning that those who benefit from the status quo would rather fight to maintain it than risk any potential cost that might come by widening their circle of compassion to include those who are marginalized. If this tendency sounds like the opposite of Jesus' message, well, that's because it is.

Perhaps it is fitting, then, to dust off the old evangelical cliché and ask, what would Jesus do about the situation in Charleston?

What if the Kanawha County Health Department had refused to yield to the political pressure to close their syringe service program in the first place? How many lives would have been saved?

What if the Charleston Police Department had made more of an effort to build bridges to the most vulnerable members of its community—the very people whom their officers are sworn to serve and protect—instead of viewing them as criminals whose drug use must be prevented at all costs, even if it means perpetuating an HIV outbreak?

What if the city council had humbled themselves enough to learn from the lived experience of people on the streets and the insight of experts in the field? How much human suffering could they have curtailed?

Alas, however, at the time of this writing, Charleston remains embroiled in the throes of a needless political battle. Preventable diseases are spreading while the overdose crisis rages on like an unchecked wildfire. In January 2022, SOAR documented 100 new infections related to IV drug use among folks in their care. Infections are rising in the hollers outside the city as well, where very little testing is being done. Inside city limits, they are verging on the precipice of a new syphilis outbreak.

While those in power continue to jockey for the upper hand, people in the streets continue to get sick and die.

Case Study #2 - River Valley Organizing in Portsmouth, OH

Meanwhile, on the banks of the Ohio River about 100 miles west of Charleston, the city of Portsmouth, OH is conducting a radical new experiment in community-based harm reduction. During the height of the

COVID-19 pandemic, local organizers moved their syringe program from the Public Health Department, where it had been located since opening in 2011, to a small ramshackle building on the city's east end, just two blocks away from the neighborhood where activists marched against the pill mills ten years earlier.

The property is owned by River Valley Organizing, a "multi-racial, multi-cultural working-class organization" focused on community-building in the Ohio River Valley.[11] Just down the road sits Portsmouth's famed Mitchellace building, a monstrous seven-story structure that has come to symbolize the city's economic decline as well as its potential resurgence. Once home to Portsmouth's largest manufacturer, over time the Mitchellace building became a "poverty porn" feature of national media outlets who like to describe the city as the "epicenter" of the opioid crisis in rural America.[12] The property is now being renovated by Portsmouth's largest mental health and addiction services provider.[13]

There's far more grant money flowing toward treatment than there is toward harm reduction these days, however. That nondescript, ramshackle building which is home to the SSP was never more than a two-bedroom shotgun house, the kind that was popular in the southern United States from the end of the Civil War to the 1920s. A concrete handicap ramp provides access to the front entrance. Taped to the front window and glass door are flyers with information about voter registration, COVID-related occupancy restrictions, and hours of operation.

I visit the SSP regularly to visit friends and attend community events. One day in the summer of 2021, I went specifically to conduct research. What follows are my observations from that visit.

• • • ● • ● • • •

When I enter the building, I see Jessica, better known to me as Jess, sitting on the couch in the front room. She greets me with a smile and some small talk. Jess and I have been working together over the past few years to provide Narcan at no cost to at-risk individuals who wouldn't normally grace the steps of the health department. Jess is known as the "Robin Hood" of naloxone. She acquires the life-saving overdose reversal medication wherever she can and distributes it to anyone in need, those whom she affectionately refers to as "my people."

My attention shifts to the reception desk. A gentleman sporting a camo cowboy hat is seated at the table talking to Paul, a local Episcopalian priest who volunteers at the SSP on Monday afternoons. Paul's black shirt and clerical collar immediately give him away. The man in the cowboy hat seems perfectly comfortable in his presence, though, and begins talking after I say hello, apparently resuming a conversation that my arrival interrupted.

"I don't judge anybody," he says, "but the other day I was at a local store and there were three or four of them just strewn out all over the ground."

He's talking about syringes, of course, the kind people use to shoot up. Not everyone is courteous enough to bring their used paraphernalia to the SSP for exchange, but the numbers have gone up since the program was moved to the east end earlier this year, highlighting the effectiveness of community-based intervention efforts. Abby Spears, a local harm reductionist and director of the SSP, agrees.

> Moving the SHRPS (Supportive Harm Reduction Programs and Services of Portsmouth) syringe program to the East End of Portsmouth as part of the partnership between River Valley Organizing, a local power-building nonprofit, and the Portsmouth City Health Department has been monumental. Since its move in November of 2020, there has been a steady monthly increase that has resulted in almost 700 new individuals being able to access much needed medically necessary services and resources. Individuals who are members of the syringe program can get not only sterile equipment but also

things like Naloxone/Narcan, Fentanyl test strips, harm reduction education, HIV testing and linkage to care, Hepatitis
C testing and direct linkage to treatment, STI testing and
sexual health education, and navigation services that connect
them to medical and mental healthcare, housing, food assistance, transportation, employment, and treatment if they
desire. It is a hub of education, connection, and community
without judgment, agenda, or expectation. For many, the SSP
is their only touch point for compassion and care where we
believe that agency and self-direction lead to empowered decision making.

SHRPS is one of the oldest programs in the state, started in
2011 by Bobbi Bratchett. It has grown and evolved based on
the feedback and information of those who access it. Now the
program averages 1000+ interactions per month, and much
of that is due to the change in location. Removing it from the
busy downtown meant that folks no longer felt unnecessarily
exposed and at risk. For others, it meant they could now walk
to the site instead of having to find transportation across town.
It also meant that the program could offer a window of operation that reflected the needs of the community with a mix
of day and evening hours to ensure that those who worked or
had families or other obligations could finally have access to
everything they needed.[14]

Turns out there are just as many folks in Portsmouth as there are in
Charleston who would rather die in the street than visit the health department. Like Charleston, the Portsmouth City Health Department is located
just down the road from the county courthouse and probation office. Believe
it or not, when the SSP was still located at the Health Department, some

people actually refused to go out of fear that it was a sting operation. They thought that if they showed up to exchange their old needles for new ones, police would arrest them.

Add to this fear the fact that there were many other offices located in the Health Department building besides the SSP. Local citizens were constantly coming and going to pay their water bills or attend to other business. People who use drugs don't always feel welcome in such places, regardless of how compassionate the public health workers running the harm reduction program might be. Stigma is real, and it keeps people from getting the help they need.

Jess's voice returns me to the present moment.

"I was just thinking about Christine," she says, referring to our mutual friend from chapter seven. "This time last year, she was helping me collect pictures for Overdose Awareness Day.[15] This year, she's going to be one of them."

Pursing my lips, I look down at the couch cushion. A spontaneous moment of silence passes in the space between us.

Before we can say anything else, the front door opens, and a young girl walks in. She moves immediately to the coffee table, helping herself to the meager supplies as if she had just walked into her own place. Paul says hello. She asks about a new health program in the next county, and while she's talking, a second girl enters the room. The same rhythm follows: coffee, small talk, and then business.

"We're trying to get into treatment... again," she says. "We burned our bridges at most of the local programs, so we'll see."

"So did I," Jess says, chuckling.

Jess has made the rounds working for a few local treatment centers, but none of her stints have lasted very long. Jess is a sensitive soul; when she hears other folks talk badly about "her people," or when she is forced to work within a system that puts too many barriers in front of those seeking help, her conscience compels her to head for the door. In her most recent job as a case manager, she overheard a fellow counselor referring to one of their clients as a "whore," and that was the final straw. Even though she needs the money, she won't continue working in an environment where such blatant prejudice is tolerated.

The conversation goes on as I sit listening. Paul and Jess relate their concerns about closing down recently to observe the death of a friend. They wonder how many people were impacted by the SSP being out of commission for a few days. Paul recounts a conversation he had with friends in rural Virginia who fear that their community is just now entering the phase that Portsmouth passed through a decade ago, where they are seeing a sudden rise in pain pills being sold on the streets.

My thoughts drift to the people I live among in my small neighborhood just fifteen minutes outside of Portsmouth. I wonder how these concerns would sound to them. As Paul and Jess move to switch places, allowing Jess to assume intake duties, my eyes are drawn to a poster on the wall behind the desk. The face of Malcolm X stares out at me alongside this quote:

> "We need more light about each other.
> Light creates understanding,
> Understanding creates love,
> Love creates patience,
> And patience creates unity."[16]

Paul sits down on the couch next to me, leaning back against the cushion and letting his shoulders drop. I mention the book I'm writing and how I'd like to highlight his faith-based harm reduction work. Paul is new to the Portsmouth community, having come straight out of seminary to serve his first parish in what was once known as the "pill mill capital of the world."

The first time Paul and I met for coffee, my own pastoral service was drawing to a close. Half a cup was all it took for me to recognize Paul as a fellow ally to people who use drugs. After settling into his new priestly role, he took definite steps to integrate into our community, joining the local opioid consortium, attending related events, and talking about harm reduction from the pulpit on Sundays. Eventually, he connected with the SSP. I wanted to know how his presence had been received by the clients here, especially given that big clerical collar he liked to wear around town as a high church clergyman.

"At first they put me in the back room," Paul says, motioning down the hall. "A few people definitely stopped in their tracks when they saw me."

"How so?" I ask.

"Well, one of the first times I volunteered, Abby sent someone to my room, but they stopped at the door and quickly turned to leave. Abby said, 'No, it's ok,' and they were like, 'but that's a *priest*!'"

Paul chuckles.

"Another time, something similar happened. I was out front at that point, but someone came through the door, took one look at me, and turned to leave. Luckily, there was another client in the room at the time, and when she saw that person about to leave, she said, 'No, he's cool. He's a priest, but he's one of the good ones.'"

I smile and scribble in my notebook: "*He's one of the good ones.*"

When I ask Paul what motivates him to engage in this ministry, he quickly affirms the popular harm reduction mantra.

"Just being able to meet people where they are is what's most important to me," he says. "Like I said, there has been some tension with certain folks due to what I call 'the stigma of the collar'"—he taps the band around his neck that signifies him as a faith leader— "but for the most part, people have come to accept and even trust my presence here. We've even had a few people stop by the church to be anointed for prayer."

"That's fantastic," I say, making a mental note to further explore Paul's expression, "the stigma of the collar." How ironic to think that people of faith can have the same stigma attached to them that those who use drugs receive from people of faith!

Before long, another couple walks through the front door, interrupting our conversation. I glance down at my watch and realize that another appointment is pressing upon me. Saying goodbye, I fold my notebook and start toward the door. On the way out, I hear Jess starting the next intake.

"Are you in danger right now in any way?" Jess asks, to which the woman shakes her head.

"Have you ever overdosed?"

"Yes."

"How many times?"

"A few."

And then I'm outside with the door closing behind me. A middle-aged couple stands on the sidewalk with cigarettes in hand. I nod and say hello, noting their ragged appearance and wondering what their story might be. Walking down the ramp toward my car, the thought occurs to me, *At least there's one place in town where they can get help without being judged for needing it.*

· · · ● · ● · · ·

Reflecting on my conversation with Paul later that day, I was struck by the unlikely intersection of these two worlds—faith and harm reduction. Then I remembered: the desire to explore this intersection is exactly why I wrote *Drugs and Jesus*. Paul's humble, unassuming presence at our local syringe exchange was a living embodiment of the message I hope to convey through this little jumble of carefully crafted words, just as Brooke Parker's advocacy is for the most vulnerable members of her community in Charleston, West Virginia.

While it is true that drug addiction is a real problem for millions of people across the world, the American overdose crisis is an issue all to itself. This devastating loss of life is not the result of a collective moral failure but of bad social policy. Our society is sick with multiple co-occurring disorders, and the war on people who use drugs is now responsible for the deaths of nearly one million individuals since 1999. America's marginalized population is bleeding out, and the first thing you do before treating any patient who's bleeding out is to *stop the bleeding*.

That means ending the war on drugs.

In case it's not clear to you what these case studies have to teach, let me spell out a few of the most outstanding lessons. For starters, let's acknowledge the fact that stigma shows up in many surprising ways for marginalized people. When was the last time you feared to walk into your local health department, or any public institution at all for that matter? What if your life literally depended on it?

How about the discrepancy between what Martin Luther King, Jr., called "just and unjust laws?" As children, we were taught that the line between right and wrong was clearly defined and embodied in the laws by which our society is governed. As adults, however, we came to learn—sometimes the hard way—that the moral choices facing the most vulnerable members of our communities are not always so cut and dry.

Need I go on, or can you see how the drug war is literally killing people who use drugs? Is it clear to you yet that Jesus still stands where he always has, not with the stone-throwing moralizers but with the people they would condemn to die?

We've nearly reached the end of our journey together, so allow me to bare my heart for a moment before we move into the last chapter. I don't know about you, but statistics alone—no matter how devastating—are too impersonal to sustain my motivation in any work. This is why my thoughts always drift away from the numbers toward real, flesh-and-blood human beings, toward the people I know who deserve better than the shoddy deal they are currently getting out of life.

People like Christine, who, despite entering recovery after thirty years of active addiction, just couldn't muster the strength to overcome the crushing weight of stigma following her relapse. Or Jessica, the Robin Hood of naloxone, who would put her own livelihood on the line rather than hang out with case workers who perpetuate society's judgmental stereotypes against her people. Or activists like Blyth Barnow, who boldly proclaim the good news that all lives truly do matter, including those of people who use drugs.

As I contemplate the faithful witness of these compassionate souls, each of whom are blazing new trails in the infant field of faith-based harm reduction, I can't help but wonder what revolutionary value has yet to be discovered in the uncharted space between these two incredible worlds.

Perhaps Jesus said it best. "The harvest is great, but the workers are few." [17] As we approach the end of our journey together, let us pray to the Lord of the harvest that he will send more workers into the field.

QUESTIONS FOR REFLECTION

What is your attitude toward syringe exchange programs? How has your view of such programs evolved, deepened, or been challenged by reading this chapter?

_____

_____

_____

_____

_____

_____

_____

_____

_____

_____

_____

_____

Thinking back to case study number one, what do you think could have motivated law enforcement officers to dump clean needles and other harm reduction paraphernalia into the river rather than give them to people who would benefit from their use? Will this action keep people from using drugs? What do you think the officers were afraid of?

_____

_____

_____

_____

_____

_____

_____

_____

_____

_____

_____

Reflecting on Paul's use of the phrase, "stigma of the collar," in case study number two, what do you think motivates him to keep coming back when even he is looked down upon as a member of the clergy?

_____

_____

_____

_____

_____

_____

_____

_____

_____

_____

_____

Try to place yourself in the shoes of a person who would "rather die on the street than visit their local health department." What kind of experience do you think this person must have had in their life to hold that conviction?

_____

_____

_____

_____

_____

_____

_____

_____

_____

_____

_____

_____

Eleven

FINDING YOUR LANE ON THE HARM REDUCTION HIGHWAY

Everyone hates a Sunday driver. Am I right?

I mean, come on, is there anything more infuriating than some guy wandering around town in his car, going nowhere in particular, just enjoying himself and the beautiful views of the countryside around him? Especially when you're the one stuck behind him.

In case you've never heard the term, Grammartist defines "Sunday driver" as "a person who pilots a car inexpertly, driving erratically, slowly or extremely cautiously. The term Sunday driver is derived from a practice of early automobile owners. In the 1920s and 1930s, many car owners did not depend on their automobiles for transportation. Taking a leisurely and largely aimless drive in the country on Sunday afternoon was a form of entertainment, as gasoline was cheap and abundant. Drivers who indulged in this practice were in no hurry, enraging other drivers on the road who were trying to get somewhere."[1]

It's an interesting bit of history, I suppose, but a frustrating practice, nonetheless. Now, if you happen to be one of these Sunday drivers, don't feel bad. We don't really hate you, we just hate what you do. It's a "love the sinner, hate the sin" kind of thing.

I'm just joshin' you, of course. Get it? But I'm also setting you up for an analogy. It must be the pastor in me coming out again.

Truth be told, most Christians are Sunday drivers when it comes to harm reduction. So are most faith communities. They're just out cruising around on some old country road, puttering along, enjoying the pretty scenery outside their window but not really going anywhere.

The aimlessness of the faith community in relation to harm reduction is a problem. What I've tried to do in this book is provide an on-ramp to the solution, a clear path for you and your community to move from uninvolved to involved, from uninformed prejudice (forgive me if I assume too much) to well-equipped service. Everything I've shared with you here has been toward that end.

What will your involvement look like? Ultimately, that is up to you. On the other side of this on-ramp lies the harm reduction highway. There you will find many different lanes of engagement that you, your community, and your ministry might take. I'm not here to tell you what you *should* do with the information you've learned in this book, only what you *could* do if you choose to act upon it. The possibilities are endless!

One thing I will be so bold as to say you should do, though, is to get off the back road and find your lane *somewhere*. Anything is better than nothing because, as you surely must know by now, there are too many lives hanging in the balance for the faith community to take a pass on this one. I've done my best to sound the alarm and give you the theological framework you need to get going. Once you clear the ramp and merge onto the highway, however, where you go is entirely up to you.

Having said that, let's review your options.

EXITING THE BACK ROAD

This analogy begins with the assumption that you've been cruising the back road. If you're already further along than that, then kudos to you! But we begin there, for better or for worse. The back road is the place of non-involvement. There, you're vaguely aware of the overdose crisis as a problem, but you're not intimately acquainted with anyone on the ground who is actively addressing it. You carry uninformed prejudice which perpetuates the stigma surrounding people who use drugs. You think the war on drugs is a good thing. In your mind, addiction is a moral failing.

But now you've entered the on-ramp, and your mindset is changing. You still have more questions than answers, but you can sense that something is happening inside your heart. Spiritual movement is taking place. Old paradigms are beginning to shift.

This is an exciting place to be as an individual. The first thing I would encourage you to do is stay the course. There is a wealth of information out there with which to continue educating yourself, and the need to do so will never cease. So, with all your getting, get understanding.[2] This means reading everything you can get your hands on and learning from folks who have been in the game longer than you. Imagine yourself as a student coming to learn at the feet of a teacher and start with the recommended reading list at the back of this book.

Faith in Harm Reduction is a comprehensive online resource to check out; subscribing to their newsletter is a great way to discover related books, podcasts, and webinars.[3] You'll even find a toolkit for faith leaders and communities on how to deal with matters relating to the overdose crisis.[4] Changing the public narrative about people who use drugs is one of the prime areas in which you can make a difference in this struggle, so I recommend you spend a lot of time and focus there.

Churches have often been the womb in which many of society's poets and prophets were born, and despite the current decline of western Christianity's influence in the public square, there is no reason to think this won't continue to be the case. These courageous souls are the ones who tell the stories that inform the way the rest of us relate to each other. You could be one of them.

THE CONSTRUCTION ZONE

Change never comes easily, though, especially at the community level. An individual's mindset might shift suddenly and significantly, prompting them to look for the nearest on-ramp by which they can exit the back road. Gripped with an exciting new vision of what could be, they quickly turn and set their sights toward the highway. But this is like a kayaker changing course midstream; a luxury cruise liner takes much longer to adjust its heading! And so it goes with community-wide change. You might come to the end of this book excited to transform your church's mindset, but then you exit the on-ramp only to find you have merged right into a construction zone!

If that's you, then don't fret, brave heart. The construction zone is the place of transition. It might be frustrating, being forced to crawl along at what feels like a snail's pace, but this is just how it is when dealing with old mindsets. People don't change their ways easily—in fact, most folks never change at all. So, be prepared for pushback and resistance. At least you're moving forward! And remember, there was no friction on the back road because you weren't going anywhere. Now, despite opposition, at least you can take heart in the fact that your progress is challenging the status quo.

If your church or faith community isn't ready for active involvement in harm reduction work, it can always provide indirect support for people who use drugs and those in recovery from a substance use disorder. This support can be as simple as providing meeting space for mutual support groups, such as Alcoholics Anonymous (AA) and their counterpart, Narcotics Anonymous (NA). People in recovery are always looking for ways to give back, so they might offer to mow the grass or take up love offerings in response to your congregation's generosity. Forming these relationships will help you build a bridge between the church and the recovery community.

THE PASSING LANE

Where I live, we encourage churches to adopt a "Faith Recovery Navigator" model. This means appointing someone in the congregation to act as the official "bridge" between church members and the community of people who use drugs. I admit that this title is ultimately too reductive because it implies that everyone who is using drugs are "out there" somewhere—when there are probably many people in your church who use drugs—but it's the best we've come up with so far.

The point is to have at least one person who is committed to being "in the know" when it comes to all the stuff you've read about in this book. Someone with their ear to the ground who can point others to available resources so they can become better equipped on the issue.

Having a church member function as a bridge between your group and the community of people who use drugs is essential to helping folks find their lane on the harm reduction highway. Eventually, people are going to need a point of contact on the ground who can help them move in and out of the passing lane. The passing lane is for those who are ready to move faster or farther than their current trajectory, or community, will allow.

Your local public health coalition will be an integral part of this process. Some county consortiums, like my own, might even have a faith-based sub-committee. If such a committee already exists in your area, join it; if it doesn't exist, start it.

The passing lane is facilitated primarily by *continuing personal education and deepening relationships with people who use drugs*. Underline that part if you need to, because it's important. It is vital that you never stop learning and never, ever stop listening. Learn from those who know more than you do and listen to those who possess experiences that you lack. Follow the social media accounts of marginalized individuals—black and brown people, members of the LGBTQ community, and others—who use their platforms to speak about these issues.

As you maintain this practice, you will gradually grow into a broader perspective that adds insight to insight. Consequently, your capacity to serve the most vulnerable members of your community will continue to increase.

THE EXPRESSWAY

Eventually, you may want to merge onto the expressway. The expressway is for individuals and small groups who are ready to engage in direct action. Following this impulse, you might start by hosting a small group discussion using this book as a guide. If the reflection questions at the end of each chapter are not enough to stimulate quality engagement, I would be happy to join you on a Zoom call for conversation or provide professional consultation to help facilitate your process.

Workshops and professional training events are both in order at this point. One church in my county hosted a "Recovery Talks" panel discussion, inviting clergy members from the community to come and learn from the experience of people who use drugs. This event was replicated by other churches in surrounding counties the following year. Such "listening campaigns" are important for all the reasons outlined in chapter two of this book. If effective service is your goal, then you must listen more than you speak.

Your local health department will be happy to facilitate training on how to recognize and respond to a drug overdose. Many community-based harm reduction agencies would also be eager to provide this service in partnership with your organization. Those who can will even hand out free naloxone and other life-saving tools to participants at these events.

One obvious way for your church to get involved is by hosting awareness events and memorial services for people who have been lost to an accidental overdose. Pastors and other faith leaders are already called upon to do this in various ways, as when someone in the community goes missing or dies suddenly and tragically. The Psalms contain a wealth of material that can be used to lament the untimely passing of individuals who have overdosed. Many parts of the Christian tradition can be faithfully adapted in service to those who have been impacted.

It doesn't have to be polished or pretty so long as it is sensitive to the needs of those who are grieving. You don't have to have all the answers. Just light a candle and show them that you care, for God's sake.

HIGH-OCCUPANCY VEHICLE LANE

Here is where the rubber meets the road. The high-occupancy vehicle lane is a special lane reserved for the use of carpools, vans, and buses. This is where you end up when the whole community gets involved.

Unfortunately, I must confess up front that I don't have a solid grasp on what it might look like for your entire community to get involved in harm reduction ministry, because there are so few examples from which to draw. But I have a few ideas about what it could look like, all of which are informed by the African proverb: "If you want to go fast, go alone, but if you want to go far, go together."

Your church could become a site for naloxone distribution. I know this is possible because I've helped multiple churches and faith-based organizations do so in my home state. In our case, this partnership is made possible through Ohio's Project DAWN (Deaths Avoided With Naloxone), a network of overdose education and naloxone distribution programs coordinated by the Ohio Department of Health.[5] Project DAWN was created through the tireless advocacy of people like Lisa Roberts, a registered nurse who led the marches against my city's "pill mills" back in the early days of the opioid crisis. Since the program's inception in 2012, it has grown to include more than 280 naloxone distribution sites in 72 of Ohio's 88 counties. Just think of all the lives that have been saved.

You may not have a program like this in your state, but you could. What it takes is a strong voice getting the attention of lawmakers and policy advocates at the state level. Groups like Faith in Public Life may be able to support you. Or, if you prefer, you can look up non-profit groups like Olive Branch Ministries, a faith-based harm reduction organization based in North Carolina that takes the mission of Jesus seriously enough to engage with people who use drugs.[6]

Another thing your community could do is to support the development of a local Recovery Community Organization (RCO).[7] RCOs are just like any other non-profit entity, except they are run *by* people in recovery *for* people in recovery, acting as a hub for local peer support services. It's not that all people who use drugs need treatment or would identify as being in recovery, but these organizations offer a direct point of contact between people who use drugs and the broader community, including any available harm reduction services.[8]

Many RCOs start small and need a fiscal agent from their community to help them get off the ground. Your church, or a coalition of churches in your county, could easily provide the initial framework for such an endeavor.

Whatever path of activism you choose, whether local, regional, or statewide, there is so much good work to be done that you could easily get lost in all the possibilities. The key, however, is to just start. Start where you are with what you have. Listen to the voice of the Other. Take what you learn from the margins of society and speak truth to those in power at the center. Use your platform wisely. Let your compassion for those who are suffering move you to act as Christ did. Don't be afraid to speak out boldly in the name of Jesus.

FINDING EACH OTHER AGAIN

If we really hope to contribute to the healing of our communities, then we have to look at the big picture and be willing to strike at the root of our social problems. My own state government is throwing buckets of money at the opioid crisis, yet it still ranks at the bottom of the national list for foster care funding, even as our local rosters are filled and overflowing. Social workers are underpaid and stretched thin with unrealistic obligations. Children are being taken from their parents and shipped hundreds of miles away in some cases.

Of course, everyone feels that the plight of these poor children is so sad, and they wish that more could be done to help them. Yet, when these kids grow up with unresolved trauma and start doing drugs themselves, those same well-wishers will want to ship them off to prison or let them die of an overdose in the street.

The point is simple, my friend. At some level, we are all responsible for the brokenness of our society. We allow cycles of injustice and suffering to continue because we fail to acknowledge how interconnected we all are. We fail to care for our neighbors on one end of the social spectrum—asking, like Cain, "Am I my brother's keeper?"—and then damn them for it on the other end, all the while assuring ourselves that the suffering of marginalized people is a result of their own personal choices and nothing more.

If only those poor, lost souls would just pull themselves up by their bootstraps and take responsibility for their lives, then the world wouldn't be in such a mess! At least, that's the popular narrative here in central Appalachia.

We must remember what Wendell Berry said: "People use drugs, legal and illegal, because their lives are intolerably painful or dull. They hate their work and find no rest in their leisure. They are estranged from their families and their neighbors. It should tell us something that in healthy societies drug use is celebrative, convivial, and occasional, whereas among us it is lonely, shameful, and addictive. We need drugs, apparently, because we have lost each other."[9]

We may not want to admit it, but deep down, most of us really do believe that it's "every man for himself." This fundamental disconnect with our neighbors has driven western society to the brink of collapse, and it now threatens to push us over the edge. Yet it is this sense of separation that the Gospel is meant to address. In the words of Jesus,

> "You are the light of the world—like a city on a hilltop that cannot be hidden. No one lights a lamp and then puts it under a basket. Instead, a lamp is placed on a stand, where it gives light to everyone in the house. In the same way, let your good deeds shine out for all to see, so that everyone will praise your heavenly Father."[10]

Wherever you end up on the harm reduction highway, my prayer is that you will become a beacon of light to those who have gotten lost in out-of-the-way places. May you be a channel of God's love for everyone you contact along the way. May the Holy Spirit guide you and may the healing ministry of Christ lead the people of your community back again. Back to God, back to themselves, and back to one another.

QUESTIONS FOR REFLECTION

Using the analogy in this chapter, where do you see yourself and/or your church community in relation to the harm reduction highway? Are you still cruising the backroads, or have you already taken the on-ramp?

_____

_____

_____

_____

_____

_____

_____

_____

_____

_____

_____

_____

What progress have you made while reading this book? Do you intend to further explore these concepts and/or share this message with other people? Where do you hope to go from here?

_____

_____

_____

_____

_____

_____

_____

_____

_____

_____

_____

_____

_____

TWELVE

DOES IT EVEN MATTER IF IT WORKS?

My friends in both the public health and harm reduction fields like to talk about "evidence-based practices" for good reason. With so many people dying due to outdated drug war policies rooted in moralistic paradigms and uninformed prejudice, it is vital that we turn our attention away from harmful ideologies to healthy social reforms that are proven to work.

Like those syringe service programs we talked about in chapter ten. There's a mounting body of evidence demonstrating how SSPs not only reduce the risk of a person contracting infectious diseases like HIV and Hepatitis through the distribution of clean needles, but they also increase the likelihood that people who need help with a substance use disorder will enter treatment, in some cases up to *five times* the normal rate.[1]

Hence the term, "evidence-based practice."

While I'm personally convinced that harm reduction is based on a whole lot of evidence that continues to grow with each passing year, I think for people of faith, the question of what works is not the only thing to consider. Our ultimate motivation boils down to a matter of simple faithfulness.

Christians are bound to grapple with the fact that many of their master's core teachings were not exactly practical, and when put to the test, they didn't really seem to work.

Take non-violence, for instance. Where did all that talk about loving one's enemies get Jesus? In the end, it got him hung up on a Roman cross, his movement shattered, and his disciples disillusioned. Sure, you can flip to the back of the book and see that things worked out in the end, but that's cheating. At that moment, in the middle of the fire, Jesus' method of confronting the evils of human society just didn't seem to "work" according to any plausible standard of measurement.

But that wasn't the point, was it?

From the very beginning, Jesus was clear that his task was simply to be faithful to the mission he received from his Father, which was to bear witness to the truth, calling the outcast to himself and inaugurating a new community right in the midst of the old one.

Ride or die, baby.

Faith-based harm reduction works in exactly the same way. We're not here to moralize about other people's choices or cast judgment on their worthiness. We know that it's not our place to hold folks accountable to our own personal ideals or try to hook them with an unspoken agenda hidden behind our offer to help.

No. None of that.

On the contrary, we're here simply to love our neighbors as ourselves by offering them the same amazing grace that God offers us. And we do it without condition—no strings attached. Why? *Because of our faith.* Because we believe that every life is precious and filled with unseen potential. All other appearances aside, we know that the man with a needle in his arm is Christ incognito, and we take great joy in giving him our service.

So, one more time, just for good measure, let's recap.

Maybe you've heard it said that harm reduction is just enabling people to use drugs without discrimination, but I'm telling you that the only thing harm reduction enables a person to do is stay alive (and that's a good thing).

Maybe you've thought that being pro-life is only about protecting the unborn, but in reality, it's about honoring *all* human life from the womb to the tomb, regardless of whether or not you think someone deserves it.

Maybe you've been told that society must be tough on crime in order to solve the problem of drug use and addiction, but history has proven otherwise, and now you know: the only way to win the war on drugs is to end it.

And finally, maybe you've bought into the notion there is nothing you can do to help people who struggle with drug addiction. God bless the naysayers, but I'm kindly giving you permission to believe otherwise. I wrote this book to poke and prod and remind you that, as a person of faith, you've been called to practice a radical, Christ-like love that extends far beyond the limits of mere human possibility.

This is what faith-based harm reduction is about, after all. Now you know, and now, taking your cue from Jesus, you're ready to begin your journey.

It's time to be about your Father's business.

THIRTEEN

A PRAYER FOR THOSE WHO ARE GONE

By Blyth Barnow

My love, my sibling, my parent, my friend.

Family.

You are family to me.

Your perfection is not required.

It never was.

Not to love you.

Not to grieve you.

You are, and have always been, worthy. We know the truth of you.

Your love, your contradictions, your challenge. We know your laughter and hurt and hope. We carry you with us, even now.

So today we call you by your name.

It is Beloved.

Today we allow ourselves to love you fully.

Today we allow ourselves to grieve you honestly. We miss you.

And we know that your life, was a life worth saving.

No matter your choices or your struggle. We miss you.

Because grief is born of knowing. May your memory be a flame for the way forward.

Compelling us to act as agents of resurrection,
Proclaiming loudly that every life is worth saving
And all loss is worthy of our grief.
Amen.

APPENDIX

A (VERY) BRIEF HISTORY OF HARM REDUCTION

HARM REDUCTION BEGAN IN Genesis chapter three. I bet you never knew that did you? Believe it or not, harm reduction has been part of God's heart toward humanity from the very beginning. Let's revisit that iconic scene for a moment.

"Adam and Eve have eaten from the tree of knowledge," God said. "This is bad. To ensure that they don't eat from the tree of life and live forever in their fallen state, let's send them away from the garden."[1]

Contrary to popular evangelical belief, God's decision to exile humanity from the Garden of Eden was not so much an act of judgment as it was an offering of grace. God sent them away to ensure that eventually they would find their way back to wholeness. Unfortunately, Adam and Eve had chosen to do something that was not in their best interest; fortunately, God was there to reduce the harms associated with their choice.

Isn't that a lovely way of reading the text?

THE MODERN HISTORY OF HARM REDUCTION

There is no universally accepted definition of harm reduction, but according to Harm Reduction International, it refers to "policies, programs, and practices that aim to minimize negative health, social, and legal impacts associated with drug use, drug policies, and drug laws."[2]

The first public voices to rise against the legal suppression of drug use in recent history began in the 1960s and 70s. Most Americans who were alive during that time generally refer to the era in terms of the "hippie movement," a decade of hedonistic, counter-cultural revolution that originated among young people on college campuses across the United States. History, however, tells a far more compelling story.

In the 1970s, for instance, government officials in the Netherlands began to ask new questions about drug prohibition laws in their country, having recognized the harm that was being done to citizens who used illicit substances, not so much by drugs themselves, but by the legal and social ramifications associated with their use. As drug use increased among people of every social stratum, enforcing those laws became problematic.

In response to this conundrum, officials created several commissions that allowed police and courts to re-evaluate whether strict enforcement of the nation's drug laws was, in fact, a good idea for their society overall. This approach became known as the "balance of harms."[3] Essentially, they wanted to know whether the harm inflicted by drug prohibition was worth the cost when it fell on more than just the most marginalized members of society.

What began as a trickle from the most unlikely of sources – the upper echelons of a national government – would soon find its way to the valleys of people down below. From such dubious beginnings, the paradigmatic history of harm reduction began.

THE HIV/AIDS EPIDEMIC

In 1984, American scientists discovered that one of the primary means of transmission for HIV/AIDS was intravenous drug use. As the AIDS epidemic swept the United States, it became apparent that people who injected drugs were second only to gay and bisexual men for contracting the virus. In fact, even today it is estimated that among more than 13 million people who inject illegal drugs worldwide, over half of them are infected with HIV.[4] As more people became aware of this fact in the 1980s, however, and as measures to implement safer drug use and needle sharing were implemented, the number of people newly infected with HIV/AIDS began to decline. The positive impact of harm reduction registered almost immediately.

Activists on the ground in those days were individuals who had been personally devastated by the AIDS epidemic. They struggled to articulate concepts that they knew needed to be brought to public attention. Harm reduction models existed in Europe and Australia at the time, but no organized movement had yet taken root in the United States.

Little by little, however, those early pioneers began to organize. Meetings were held in homes, where people with lived experience shared anecdotes and information. Gradually, a consensus emerged among activists that the harm reduction movement should be guided by the insights and experiences of people who were directly affected by the harms associated with drug use and drug laws. This principle, which has been adopted in many fields of social activism, is enshrined in the popular slogan that remains in use among harm reductionists today: "Nothing about us without us."

"NOTHING ABOUT US WITHOUT US"

It is difficult to say exactly where the phrase, "Nothing about us without us," originated. In the United States, it seems to have begun as a slogan of the South African disability rights movement in the 1980s. At least, that is where the disability rights activist James Charlton traced it. Before that, it probably found its way to America from labor activists in Europe, where it has since been taken up by multiple groups in the struggle for the right of self-determination.

One of the first successful efforts to organize harm reduction began in Australia in the 1980s, where activists noted that the general public health response to accidental overdose and drug-related crime was being developed without the input of people who actually used drugs. Acknowledging that this disparity was both ethically and practically problematic, officials began making efforts to include and support this part of the population in public policy decisions.

Since then, researchers have concluded that the existence of "user groups" helps to significantly reduce the spread of HIV among people who use drugs.[5] The harm reduction principle of following "evidence-based practices" can be traced to these early successes. In short, harm reduction works. In fact, it works to such a degree that some people regard it as simple common sense.

A COMMONSENSE APPROACH TO PUBLIC HEALTH

Following the release of my first book, *The Face of Addiction*, I was contacted by a fellow author in the UK who was drawn to a statement I made on social media that "harm reduction is a pro-life issue." We scheduled a Zoom call to discuss our respective works, mine on the opioid crisis and his on video gaming. He was a lovely fellow, and I walked away from our conversation with a deep appreciation for his mission to help kids develop healthy video game habits.[6]

When I talked about the need for harm reduction and criminal justice reform in America, however, his response was quite casual. "Oh, you mean things like methadone treatment and supervised injection sites," he said. Not only did his response to my "radical" ideas lack the element of genuine surprise, but he also seemed thoroughly unimpressed. Not because he disliked or disagreed with my conviction, but because to him, these ideas were nothing new. Upon further reflection, I realized that geography had a lot to do with it.

As a general philosophy, harm reduction is far more accepted in places like the UK, where public health has taken precedence over punishment since the Merseyside Model was first developed in Liverpool in the 1970s.[7] Countries like the UK, Netherlands, and Portugal have achieved notable improvements in the overall health of their citizens, including decreasing rates of addiction and overdose, by enacting social policy reforms that prioritize harm reduction over incarceration.

In the UK, harm reduction represents a commonsense approach to public health. In America, it remains a radical idea whose day has not yet fully dawned. Perhaps it's time we learn a thing or two from our neighbors across the pond.

HARM REDUCTION AS A SOCIAL MOVEMENT

To sum up the history of harm reduction in a single chapter is impossible. Even an entire book would fail to do the trick, as Maia Salavitz makes clear in the beginning of her groundbreaking work, *Undoing Drugs: The Untold History of Harm Reduction and the Future of Addiction*. If anything you've read here piques your curiosity about this burgeoning movement, then by all means, go read her book. Before you do, however, allow me to drive home my final point, which was really my first point, one last time.

Before it ever gained traction among public health institutions, harm reduction emerged as a radical critique of unjust social and legal systems, born from the struggle and suffering of marginalized people in response to harmful policies based on prohibitionist ideals. In many ways, the clash was inevitable. Harm reduction was destined to either collapse those policies or be integrated into them.

At the height of the AIDS epidemic, when medical professionals recognized the limitations of the legal system as an appropriate response to public health needs, they began working with harm reductionists to keep people safe by going around the law, providing criminal paraphernalia such as syringes and condoms to at-risk individuals.[8] Advocating for a more humane approach, they started referring to affected individuals in terms of group identity, such as the "community of people who use drugs." By presenting a collective identity to the public consciousness, health workers were able to apply more pressure on elected officials to address policies and practices that were harming people in those groups.

This strategy was effective because it demonstrated the vital connection between individuals in these groups and the broader community. As the general public came to understand how meeting the specific health needs of the gay community would in turn protect *them* from the risks associated with HIV transmission through intravenous drug use, they quickly warmed up to the idea of harm reduction. As ironic as it sounds, collective benefits *can* arise from petty self-interest. Solidarity forever.

So, it was the spread of HIV/AIDS that initially brought harm reduction to the mainstream of public health. Prior to that time, harm reductionists were focused just as much on social injustices as they were on the medical needs of individuals. The absorption of harm reduction into the public health field may have changed the overall dynamic, but the voices of marginalized people continue to call for justice.

Maybe I've beat this drum to death by now but let me say it one more time. From the beginning of his ministry on Earth, Jesus urged his disciples to pay attention to the wisdom found in the experience of the Other, those who were marginalized by the prevailing culture. Through the advocacy of the Holy Spirit, that work is still going on today. Whatever you choose to do in response to their voice is up to you. All I'm asking is that you put your ear to the ground and listen.

GLOSSARY

BIOPSYCHOSOCIAL MODEL - A multifaceted conceptualization that understands addiction to be the result of a constellation of factors, rather than a single underlying cause, which make a person susceptible to substance use disorder.[1]

Fentanyl - A powerful synthetic opioid that is like morphine but 50 to 100 times more potent. It is a prescription drug that is also made and used illegally. Like morphine, it is a medicine that is typically used to treat patients with severe pain, especially after surgery. It is also sometimes used to treat patients with chronic pain who are physically tolerant to other opioids.[2]

Fentany test strip (FTS) - A simple, inexpensive, and evidence-based method of averting drug overdose. FTS are small strips of paper that can detect the presence of fentanyl in any drug batch—pills, powder, or injectables. This tool might be lifesaving for the teenager experimenting for the first time, the individual in the throes of a severe opioid use disorder, the concertgoer looking for a trip, the person using a preferred substance obtained from a new source, or the individual years into recovery. FTS also support the dignity and well-being of people who use drugs (PWUD), enabling them to make educated decisions about their safety.[3]

Harm reduction - A set of practical strategies and ideas aimed at reducing negative consequences associated with drug use and drug laws. Harm Reduction is also a movement for social justice built on a belief in, and respect for, the rights of people who use drugs.[4]

Hot shot - An intentionally lethal dose of a drug that is introduced into the body by way of intravenous injection.[5]

Naloxone - A medication approved by the Food and Drug Administration (FDA) designed to rapidly reverse opioid overdose. It is an opioid antagonist—meaning that it binds to opioid receptors and can reverse and block the effects of other opioids, such as heroin, morphine, oxycodone, and fentanyl. It can be administered as a nasal spray or injected into the muscle, under the skin, or into the veins.

NARCAN®[6] - The popular brand name of the prescription medicine naloxone which is administered via nasal spray.

Opioid - A class of substances that include heroin, synthetic opioids such as fentanyl, and pain relievers available legally by prescription, such as oxycodone (OxyContin®), hydrocodone (Vicodin®), codeine, morphine, and many others. All opioids are chemically related and interact with opioid receptors on nerve cells in the body and brain.[7]

Overdose - A biological response to conditions that result when the human body receives too much of a certain substance or mix of substances. An overdose can be intentional or accidental. People can overdose on illicit drugs, alcohol, prescription medications, and many other substances. In many cases, overdoses are fatal, although most individuals who have overdosed can be saved if medical treatment is provided quickly enough.[8] For more information on how to recognize and respond to an opioid overdose,

visit https://harmreduction.org/issues/overdose-prevention/overview/over
dose-basics/recognizing-opioid-overdose.

Overdose crisis - Often used interchangeably with "opioid crisis" of "opioid
epidemic," this term refers to the growing number of deaths and hospitaliza-
tions from opioids, including both prescription and illicit drugs. In recent
years, death rates from these drugs have skyrocketed to over 90,000 a year, or
246 a day, across the U.S. Drug overdose is now the leading cause of accidental
death in the United States, largely due to the opioid epidemic.[9]

Pill mill - A place where doctors hand out prescriptions for drugs (usually
opiate painkillers), in an unethical or illegal fashion.[10] Pill mills became the
focal point of media attention during the early days of the modern opioid
crisis. When law enforcement began to crack down on their operations, the
illicit drug market gave way to street heroin, which was cheaper and easier to
obtain.

Psychoactive drug - A chemical substance that acts primarily upon the
central nervous system where it alters brain function, resulting in temporary
changes in perception, mood, consciousness, and behavior.[11]

Recovery - The definition of being "in recovery" from substance use disorder
varies from one person and organization to the next. The broadest and most
accessible definition was originally put forth by Dan Biggs, director of the
Chicago Recovery Alliance, who defined recovery simply as "any positive
change as a person defines it for him/herself."[12] A 2015 NIH-funded study
called "What Is Recovery?," published in the Journal of Studies on Alcohol
and Drugs, provides an empirically-derived definition of recovery based on
how it is experienced by those who actually live it. For more information, visit https://www.asam.org/Quality-Science/publications/magazine/read/arti
cle/2015/04/10/what-is-recovery.

Safe injection site - Legally sanctioned facilities that allow people to consume pre-obtained drugs under the supervision of trained staff. Supervised consumption services (SCS) are designed to reduce the health and public order issues often associated with public drug consumption. They are also called overdose prevention centers, safe or supervised injection facilities (SIFs), and drug consumption rooms (DCRs).[13]

Substance use disorder (SUD) - A complex condition in which there is uncontrolled use of a substance despite harmful consequences. People with SUD have an intense focus on using a certain substance(s) such as alcohol, tobacco, or illicit drugs, to the point where the person's ability to function in day to day life becomes impaired. People keep using the substance even when they know it is causing or will cause problems. The most severe SUDs are sometimes called addictions.[14]

Syringe service program (SSP) - Community-based prevention programs that can provide a range of services, including linkage to substance use disorder treatment, access to and disposal of sterile syringes and injection equipment, and vaccination, testing, and linkage to care and treatment for infectious diseases.[15]

War on drugs - A government-led initiative based on prohibitionist ideals that aims to stop illegal drug use, distribution, and trade by dramatically increasing prison sentences for both drug dealers and users.[16] For a brief history of the drug war, visit https://drugpolicy.org/issues/brief-history-drug-war.

RECOMMENDED READING

This is Ohio: The Overdose Crisis and the Front Lines of a New America by Jack Shuler

Dreamland: The True Tale of America's Opiate Epidemic by Sam Quinones

The Least of Us: True Tales of America and Hope in the Time of Fentanyl and Meth by Sam Quinones

Unbroken Brain: A Revolutionary New Way of Understanding Addiction by Maia Szalavitz

Undoing Drugs: The Untold Story of Harm Reduction by Maia Szalavitz

Fentanyl, Inc.: How Rogue Chemists are Creating the Deadliest Wave of the Opioid Epidemic by Ben Westhoff

Dopesick: Dealers, Doctors, and the Drug Company that Addicted America by Beth Macy

Drug Use for Grown Ups: Chasing Liberty in the Land of Fear by Dr. Carl Hart

The Face of Addiction: Stories of Loss and Recovery by Joshua Lawson

Never Enough: The Neuroscience and Experience of Addiction by Judith Grisel

Chasing the Scream: The First and Last Days of the War on Drugs by Johann Hari

American Overdose: The Opioid Tragedy in Three Acts by Chris McGreal

In the Realm of Hungry Ghosts: Close Encounters with Addiction by Gabor Mate

Fighting for Space: How a Group of Drug Users Transformed One City's Struggle with Addiction by Travis Lupick

Globalization of Addiction: A Study in Poverty of Spirit by Bruce Alexander

REFERENCES

ADDICTION CENTER. (N.D.). *OVERDOSE*. Addiction Center. Retrieved April 15, 2022, from https://www.addictioncenter.com/drugs/overdose/

Addition Center. (n.d.). *The Opioid Epidemic*. Addiction Center. Retrieved April 15, 2022, from https://www.addictioncenter.com/opiates/opioid-epidemic/

American Psychiatric Association. (n.d.). *Psychiatry.org - What Is A Substance Use Disorder?* Retrieved April 15, 2022, from https://www.psychiatry.org/patients-families/addiction/what-is-addiction

AP. (2021, March 9). *West Virginia Senate Passes Syringe Exchange Regulation Bill*. AP NEWS. https://apnews.com/article/charleston-bills-west-virginia-4e3f8b5d71e74a0700be50d3706985c3

Appel, G., Farmer, B., & Avery, J. (2021). *Fentanyl Test Strips Empower People And Save Lives—So Why Aren't They More Widespread?* https://doi.org/10.1377/forefront.20210601.974263

Berry, W. (2003). *The Art of the Commonplace: The Agrarian Essays of Wendell Berry* (N. Wirzba, Ed.). Counterpoint.

Bonhoeffer, D. (2009). *Life Together: The Classic Exploration of Faith in Community*. Harper Collins.

CDC. (n.d.-a). *America's Drug Overdose Epidemic: Data To Action*. Centers For Disease Control And Prevention . Retrieved February 19, 2022, from https://www.cdc.gov/injury/features/prescription-drug-overdose/index.html

CDC. (n.d.-b). *Syringe Services Programs (SSPs) | CDC*. Centers for Disease Control and Prevention. Retrieved April 15, 2022, from https://www.cdc.gov/ssp/index.html

City of Charleston. (n.d.). *Welcome To Charleston, West Virginia*. Retrieved February 20, 2022, from https://www.charlestonwv.gov/

Clark, H. W., & Corbett, J. M. (1993). Needle exchange programs and social policy. *The Journal of Mental Health Administration, 20*(1), 66–71. https://doi.org/10.1007/BF02521404

Comer Family Foundation. (2013, November 18). *Two Decades Of Positive Change: A Brief History Of The Harm Reduction Coalition - Comer Family Foundation*. https://www.comerfamilyfoundation.org/articles/two-decades-of-positive-change-a-brief-history-of-the-harm-reduction-coalition

Counseling Center, Inc. (2021, February 1). *The Counseling Center's New Campus: FAQ's The Counseling Center*. The Counseling Center. https://thecounselingcenter.org/2021/02/the-counseling-centers-new-campus-faqs/

Drug Policy Alliance. (n.d.-a). *Making Economic Sense*. Drug Policy Alliance. Retrieved February 19, 2022, from https://drugpolicy.org/issues/making-economic-sense

Drug Policy Alliance. (n.d.-b). *Overdose Prevention Centers*. Drug Policy. Retrieved April 15, 2022, from https://drugpolicy.org/issues/supervised-consumption-services

Durant, W. (1963). *The story of civilization*. Fine Communications.

Eli, P. (20217-7-5). *The Pill Mill That Ravaged Portsmouth - Cincinnati Magazine*. Cincinnati Magazine. https://www.cincinnatimagazine.com/features/pill-mill-portsmouth/

Faces & Voices of Recovery. (2019, November 23). *RCO Best Practices*. Faces & Voices Of Recovery. https://facesandvoicesofrecovery.org/rco-best-practices/

Fields, B. (2007, July 16). *Pill mill doctor wants to go home*. https://www.dailyindependent.com/news/local_news/pill-mill-doctor-wants-to-go-home/article_db1a61eb-ab99-5c4d-a2bb-b663c2c7c874.html

Florence, C. S., Zhou, C., Luo, F., & Xu, L. (2016). *The Economic Burden of Prescription Opioid Overdose, Abuse, and Dependence in the United States, 2013. 54*(10), 901–906. https://doi.org/10.1097/MLR.0000000000000625

Fox, M. (2021, July 14). *Drug Overdose Deaths In 2020 Hit Highest Number Ever Recorded, CDC Data Shows | CNN.* CNN. https://www.cnn.com/2021/07/14/health/drug-overdose-deaths-2020/index.html

Gill, N. S. (2019, February 18). *Enuma Elish: The Oldest Written Creation Myth.* Learn Religions. https://www.learnreligions.com/enuma-elish-the-oldest-written-creation-myth-117858

Giordano, A. L. (2021, July 10). *What Exactly Is The Biopsychosocial Model Of Addiction?* Psychology Today. https://www.psychologytoday.com/us/blog/understanding-addiction/202107/what-exactly-is-the-biopsychosocial-model-addiction

Grammarist. (n.d.). *Sunday Driver.* GRAMMARIST. Retrieved April 15, 2022, from https://grammarist.com/interesting-words/sunday-driver/

Hagan, H., McGough, J. P., Thiede, H., Hopkins, S., Duchin, J., & Alexander, E. R. (2000). Reduced injection frequency and increased entry and retention in drug treatment associated with needle-exchange participation in Seattle drug injectors. *Journal of Substance Abuse Treatment, 19*(3), 247–252. https://doi.org/10.1016/s0740-5472(00)00104-5

Harm Reduction International. (n.d.). *What Is Harm Reduction?* Harm Reduction International. Retrieved April 15, 2022, from https://www.hri.global/what-is-harm-reduction

Hart, C. L. (2021). *Drug Use for Grown-Ups*. Penguin Press.

History. (2017, May 31). *War On Drugs*. HISTORY. https://www.history.com/topics/crime/the-war-on-drugs

Hyden, D. H. (2020). *The Sober Addict*. True 2 Scale.

Jürgens, R. (2008). *"Nothing about us without us" — Greater, meaningful involvement of people who use illegal drugs: A public health, ethical, and human rights imperative, International edition*. Canadian HIV/AIDS Legal Network . https://www.opensocietyfoundations.org/uploads/b99c406f-5e45-4474-9343-365e548daade/nothing-about-us-without-us-report-20080501.pdf

King, Jr., M. L. (1967, April 4). *Beyond Vietnam - A Time to Break Silence*.

Lawson, J. (2021). *The Face of Addiction: Stories of Loss and Recovery*. Quoir.

Mann, B. (2021, June 17). *Needle Exchanges, Access To Safer Narcotics Could Save Lives — But It's A Tough Sell*. NPR.Org. https://www.npr.org/2021/06/17/1007805678/needle-exchanges-access-to-safer-narcotics-could-save-lives-but-its-a-tough-sell?

Mulvaney, K. (2021, July 7). *RI Gov. McKee Signs Legislation Allowing Safe-injection Sites Into Law*. The Providence Journal.

https://www.providencejournal.com/story/news/2021/07/07/
gov-mckee-signs-legislation-allowing-safe-injection-sites-into-
law/7891057002/

National Association of Counties. (2019, May). *Opioids in Appalachia:
The Role of Counties in Reversing a Regional Epidemic.*
https://www.naco.org/sites/default/files/documents/Opioids-Full.pdf

National Institute on Drug Abuse. (n.d.). *Opioids | National Institute On
Drug Abuse.* National Institute On Drug Abuse. Retrieved April 15, 2022,
from https://nida.nih.gov/drug-topics/opioids

NIH. (2021, March 11). *Opioid Overdose Crisis | National Institute On Drug
Abuse.* National Institute On Drug Abuse. https://nida.nih.gov/drug-
topics/opioids/opioid-overdose-crisis

Ohio Department of Health. (n.d.). *Project DAWN.* Ohio.Gov. Retrieved
April 15, 2022, from https://odh.ohio.gov/know-our-programs/violence-
injury-prevention-program/projectdawn/

Olive Branch Ministry. (n.d.). *Faith-based Harm Reduction.* Olive Branch
Ministry. Retrieved April 15, 2022,
from https://olivebranchministry.org/

Parker, B. (2021, June 10). *Personal Communication*
[Letter to Joshua Lawson].

Peace, L. (2020, December 15). *Behind Charleston, West Virginia's HIV
Outbreak.* Mountain State Spotlight. https://mountainstatespotlight.
org/2020/12/15/when-a-west-virginia-county-eliminated-its-needle-
exchange-experts-forewarned-of-an-hiv-crisis-now-its-here/

Peace, L. (2021, February 11). *The CDC Says Kanawha County's HIV Outbreak Is The Most Concerning In The United States - Mountain State Spotlight*. Mountain State Spotlight. https://mountainstatespotlight.org/2021/02/11/the-cdc-says-kanawha-countys-hiv-outbreak-is-the-most-concerning-in-the-united-states/

Perez, D. (2022, February 7). *Meet Them Where They Are—What It Means In 2021*. Wild Simple Joy. https://wildsimplejoy.com/meet-them-where-they-are/

Poellot, E. (n.d.). *Spirit Of Harm Reduction: A Toolkit For Communities Of Faith Facing Overdose - National Harm Reduction Coalition*. National Harm Reduction Coalition. Retrieved April 15, 2022, from https://harmreduction.org/issues/harm-reduction-basics/spirit-of-harm-reduction-a-toolkit-for-communities-of-faith-facing-overdose/

Poverty Porn: What Is It And How To Avoid It? (2021, July 19). Wiki Impact. https://www.wikiimpact.com/poverty-porn-what-is-it-and-how-to-avoid-it/

Psychoactive Drug. (n.d.). ScienceDaily. Retrieved April 15, 2022, from https://www.sciencedaily.com/terms/psychoactive_drug.htm

Raby, J. (2021, April 21). *CDC: West Virginia HIV Wave Could Be 'tip Of The Iceberg.'* AP NEWS. https://apnews.com/article/opioids-coronavirus-pandemic-drug-abuse-west-virginia-charleston d825c1b710923c1ef636f21f4b349a71

Ren. (2020, April 22). *The Threat Of "Pill Mills" In America*. Narconon
Ojai. https://www.narcononojai.org/blog/the-threat-of-pill-mills-in-
america.html

Robertson, A. (2021). *Taming Gaming*. Unbound Publishing.

RVO. (n.d.). *River Valley Organizing - About Us*. Retrieved February 20,
2022,from https://www.rivervalleyorganizing.org/about-us

Sarosi, P. (2010, May 31). *Liverpool: Back To The Roots Of Harm Reduction
- Drugreporter*. Drugreporter. https://drogriporter.hu/en/liverpool-
back-to-the-roots-of-harm-reduction/

Slayton, N. (2021, May 21). *Time To Retire The Word 'Homeless' And Opt
For 'Houseless' Or 'Unhoused' Instead?* Architectural Digest.
https://www.architecturaldigest.com/story/homeless-unhoused

Solzhenitsyn, A. (1997, January 30). *The Gulag Archipelago, 1918-1956:
An Experiment In Literary Investigation (Volume One)*. Basic Books.

Spears, A. (n.d.). *Response to SHRPS* [Letter to Joshua Lawson].

Statista. (n.d.). *Legal Abortions Number U.S. 1973-2019 | Statista*. Statista.
Retrieved February 19, 2022, from https://www.statista.com/statistics/
185274/number-of-legal-abortions-in-the-us-since-2000/

Stixx, N. (2019, March 21). *Urban Dictionary: Hot-shot*. Urban Dictionary.
https://www.urbandictionary.com/define.php?term=hot-shot

Szalavitz, M. (2017). *Unbroken Brain: A Revolutionary New Way of Understanding Addiction*. Picador.

Volpe, D. A., Tobin, G. A. M., Mellon, R. D., Katki, A. G., Parker, R. J., Colatsky, T., Kropp, T. J., & Verbois, S. L. (2011). Uniform assessment and ranking of opioid Mu receptor binding constants for selected opioid drugs. *Regulatory Toxicology and Pharmacology, 59*(3), 385–390. https://doi.org/10.1016/j.yrtph.2010.12.007

Westhoff, B. (2019). *Fentanyl, Inc.: How Rogue Chemists Are Creating the Deadliest Wave of the Opioid Epidemic*. Atlantic Monthly Press.

WV Health Right Inc. (n.d.). Retrieved February 20, 2022, from https://wvhealthright.org/

X, M. (1964, August 25). *Racism: The Cancer That is Destroying America*. Egyptian Gazette.

END NOTES

CHAPTER 1

1 See Philip Eli's article "The Pill Mill that Ravaged Portsmouth."

2 Fields, 2007.

3 National Association of Counties, 2019.

4 *Dopesick* by Beth Macy and *Dreamland* by Sam Quinones.

5 Lawson, 2021.

6 Bonhoeffer, 2009.

7 Corinthians 3:11.

8 Galatians 4:15.

9 Matthew 25:40.

CHAPTER 2

1 Matthew 15:24.

2 1 Samuel 17:43.

3 Matthew 15:26.

4 Matthew 15:27

5 Matthew 8:8-10.

6 Matthew 8:10.

7 Romans 2:17-19.

8 Amos 9:7.

9 Amos 9:11; Acts 15:16-18.

CHAPTER 3

1 For more faith-based resources, check out https://femminary.com/materials.

CHAPTER 4

1 Romans 5:8.

2 1 John 4:19.

3 John 15:16.

4 Perez, 2022.

5 Luke 10:27.

6 About a day's worth of wages.

7 Luke 10:30-35.

CHAPTER 6

1 Solzhenitsyn, 1997.

2 Florence et al., 2016.

3 CDC, n.d.

4 Statista, n.d.

5 NIH, 2021.

6 Psalm 139:14 (NIV).

CHAPTER 7

1 Matthew 23:13.

2 Gill, 2019.

3 Multiple references, starting with Genesis 1:3.

4 Romans 4:17; Hebrews 11:3.

5 Matthew 15:28.

6 Isaiah 29:13.

CHAPTER 8

1 From his 1967 speech at NYC Riverside Church entitled "Beyond Vietnam," one year to the day before he was assassinated.

2 Drug Policy Alliance, n.d.

3 Public Enemy Number One: A Pragmatic Approach to America's Drug Problem. (nixonfounda‌tion.org).

4 Durant, 1963.

5 For an eye-opening look at how this process unfolds, check out Ben Westhoff's groundbreaking book, *Fentanyl, Inc.*

6 Mulvaney, 2021.

7 For more info, read *Drug Use for Grown Ups* by Dr. Carl Hart.

8 Giordan, 2021.

9 Matthew 5:9 (NIV).

CHAPTER 9

1 Fox, 2021.

2 Mann, 2021.

CHAPTER 10

1 City of Charleston, n.d.

2 Peace, 2021.

3 Raby, 2021.

4 Peace, 2021.

5 AP, 2021.

6 B. Parker, personal communication, June 10, 2021.

7 AP, 2021.

8 WV Health Right Inc, n.d.

9 Slayton, 2021.

10 Raby, 2021.

11 RVO, n.d.

12 *Poverty Porn: What Is It And How To Avoid It?*, 2021.

13 Spears, n.d.

14 Counseling Center, Inc., 2021.

15 See https://www.overdoseday.com/ for more details.

16 X, 1964.

17 Matthew 9:37.

CHAPTER 11

1 Grammarist, n.d.

2 Proverbs 4:7.

3 Find it here: https://harmreduction.org/our-work/action/faith-in-harm-reduction/.

4 Poellot, n.d.

5 Ohio Department of Health, n.d.

6 Olive Branch Ministry, n.d.

7 Faces & Voices of Recovery, 2019.

8 For an example of all the wonderful possibilities that might arise from the presence of an RCO in

your community, check out the Hope Recovery Community in Medina, Ohio.

9 Berry, 2003.

10 Matthew 5:14.

CHAPTER 12

1 Hagan et al., 2000.

APPENDIX

1 Genesis 3:22-23a, paraphrased.

2 Harm Reduction International, n.d.

3 Harm Reduction International, n.d.

4 Jürgens, 2008.

5 Jürgens, 2008.

6 Robertson, 2021.

7 Sarosi, 2010.

8 Clark & Corbett, 1993.

GLOSSARY

1 Giordano, 2021.

2 Volpe et al., 2011.

3 Appel et al., 2021.

4 Harm Reduction International, n.d.

5 Stixx, 2019.

6 Visit https://www.narcan.com/ for more details.

7 National Institute on Drug Abuse, n.d.

8 Addiction Center, n.d.

9 Addiction Center, n.d.

10 Ren, 2020.

11 Psychoactive Drug, n.d.

12 Comer Family Foundation, 2013.

13 Drug Policy Alliance, n.d.

14 American Psychiatric Association, n.d.

15 CDC, n.d.

16 History, 2017.

For more information about Joshua Lawson,
or to contact him for speaking engagements,
please visit www.lawsonwrites.com.

Many Voices. One Message.

For more information, please visit
www.quoir.com